"In poignant reflections on that the journey of faith is o~~~~~ ~~~ ~ ~~~~~ and large obediences to the often tender, sometimes demanding, but always faithful promptings of the Spirit. Every Christ-follower committed to the journey of faith will benefit from Dunning's clear message that while the destination is important, what we become as we go is essential."

—**David Busic**
President
Nazarene Theological Seminary

"Rarely does one find a text that so capably integrates solid biblical exposition, theological reflection, and faith formation from the reader's own Christian pilgrimage. Through a series of studies in the narratives of Abraham's journey, Dunning brings the reader into an engaging and transforming dialogue with the biblical text, key tenets of the Christian faith, and the life of holiness. This text demonstrates a depth and a breadth much needed in the church today. *Abraham: The Tests of Faith* will serve both as a trustworthy theological commentary on the biblical text and as a challenge to the Christian who seeks maturity of faith."

—**Timothy M. Green**
Dean of the School of Religion and
Professor of Old Testament Literature and Theology
Trevecca Nazarene University

"The well-respected, seasoned theologian H. Ray Dunning helps us to discover from the narrative of Abraham that in the inevitable tests of life God will be faithful and we can be people of faith. These truths are preachable . . . teachable . . . and livable by faith."

—**Nina G. Gunter**
General Superintendent Emerita
Church of the Nazarene

"Ray Dunning has reflected on the life of Abraham through experienced eyes, seasoned biblical study, and down-to-earth life lessons. The holy life, he concludes, is shaped in our response to the voice that calls us and the life situations that confront us. At the end, what we know best is not where we arrived but who God is."

—**Dan Boone**
President
Trevecca Nazarene University

"Here is a biblically centered, theologically sound, and practical book, which in this case takes a careful, new look at Abraham's journey of faith. I commend this book to all who are looking for a firmly Wesleyan study that will challenge the commitment of all believers everywhere."

—**Kevin M. Ulmet**
Senior Pastor
Nashville First Church of the Nazarene

ABRAHAM
The Tests of Faith

H. RAY DUNNING

BEACON HILL PRESS
OF KANSAS CITY

Copyright 2012 by H. Ray Dunning

ISBN 978-0-8341-2880-4

Printed in the
United States of America

Cover Design: J.R. Caines
Interior Design: Sharon Page

All Scripture quotations not otherwise designated are from the *New Revised Standard Version* (NRSV) of the Bible, copyright 1989 by the Division of Christian Education of the National Council of the Churches of Christ in the USA. Used by permission. All rights reserved.

Permission to quote from the following copyrighted versions of the Bible is acknowledged with appreciation:

The New Testament in Modern English (PHILLIPS), Revised Student Edition, by J. B. Phillips, translator. Copyright 1958, 1960, 1972 by J. B. Phillips.

The *Revised Standard Version* (RSV) of the Bible, copyright 1946, 1952, 1971 by the Division of Christian Education of the National Council of the Churches of Christ in the USA.

The Message (TM). Copyright © 1993. Used by permission of NavPress Publishing Group.

Scripture quotations marked KJV are from the King James Version.

Library of Congress Cataloging-in-Publication Data

Dunning, H. Ray, 1926-
   Abraham : the tests of faith / H. Ray Dunning.
     p. cm.
   Includes bibliographical references (p.   ).
   ISBN 978-0-8341-2880-4 (pbk.)
 1. Abraham (Biblical patriarch) 2. Bible. O.T. Genesis—Criticism, interpretation, etc. 3. Faith. I. Title.
   BS580.A3D86 2012
   222'.11092—dc23

2012020363

Dedicated to the congregation of the
Camden, Tennessee, Church of the Nazarene,
with whom I first shared these studies
while serving as their interim pastor

CONTENTS

Introduction	9
1. The Test of Discipleship	21
2. The Test of Integrity	31
3. The Test of Self-Interest	39
4. The Test of Forgiveness	47
5. The Test of Faith, Part 1	51
6. The Test of Faith, Part 2	61
7. The Test of the Vultures	65
8. The Test of the Dark Night	73
9. The Test of Patience	79
10. The Test of Holy Living	85
11. The Test of Compassion	93
12. The Test of Total Commitment	99
13. Preserving the Faith	107
Epilogue	113
Notes	117
Bibliography	125

Know ye therefore that they which are of faith,
the same are the children of Abraham.
—Gal. 3:7 (KJV)

INTRODUCTION

God's redemptive activity on behalf of the human race took a significant change of direction with the call of a middle-aged man who lived in ancient Mesopotamia. His name was Abram. Genesis 1—11 implies that up to that time God had acted without mediation. These eleven chapters do two things: (1) they answer the question of why the human race is in such a predicament—seeking but never finding lasting happiness, and (2) they picture the Creator endeavoring to make people aware of their need and attempting to create barriers to their further unhappiness.[1] Genesis 3:9 records the Lord God speaking directly to Adam and Eve, asking the question, "Where are you?" in an effort to elicit the sense of need required for restoration. In general, God apparently used the stimulus of conscience to guide the human race in living out his creative intention for it.

The great flood of Noah's day was an act of judgment resulting from the reversal of creation, not just a punishment for the sin of the flood generation. As Joseph Blenkinsopp put it, "The world in which order first arose out of a primeval watery chaos is now reduced to the watery chaos out of which it arose—chaos-come-again."[2] Thus the pattern could be seen as moving from creation to uncreation and then to re-creation. The words of Gen. 6:12 that "all flesh had corrupted its way upon earth" suggest that natural laws had been broken by all levels of created beings and that the orderly work of creation had been dissolved.[3] The flood could be viewed as an attempt not only to bring the human race back to its original destiny but also to restore creation to its original order. Although deeply sorry he had created humans, God did not totally destroy them but found one righteous man who was the agent in this second attempt at a paradise. However, all this was to no avail, as the postflood events in Noah's immediate family demonstrated and the incident of the Tower of Babel validated.

Two of the major interpreters of Gen. 1—11, Gerhard von Rad and Claus Westermann, emphasize that while these chapters reflect the spread of sin and the intensification of moral evil, the structure also emphasizes that each major violation of the order God intended for the human race was accompanied by the manifestation of grace. Each transgression resulted in the declaration of judgment, but in each case, they point out, the punishment is lessened. This pattern is so pervasive that, following the insights of von Rad and Westermann, David Clines suggests that one can inscribe over this prepatriarchal history the words of Paul: "Where sin increased, grace abounded all the more" (Rom. 5:20).[4]

On the surface, God does not seem to manifest his grace by the lessening of the punishment following the ill-fated attempt at building a secular city (Babylon), whose tower served as a brash monument to an alternative religion. Nevertheless, if we recognize that the break at chapter 12 was not original, the call of Abram was the most dramatic and obvious of all the manifestations of grace.

With the awakening of Abram and his call, God was choosing a partner in this redemptive enterprise. Abram himself was to be a recipient of God's blessing, but in this position he was to be not only the model of the Lord's creative intention for humanity but also the source of the family through whom God intended to put the world to rights. By living out the divine design, Abram could provide what an abstract voice and the guidance of conscience could never adequately do. This "election" purpose was expressed in the outcome of Abram's faithful response to God's call, "In you all the families of the earth shall be blessed" (v. 3).[5] In making this same point, N. T. Wright refers to a Jewish tradition based on Gen. 12 that said, "Abraham will be God's means of undoing the sin of Adam." Wright adds,

> Thus at key moments—Abraham's call, his circumcision, the offering of Isaac, the transition from Abraham to Isaac, and from Isaac to Jacob, and in the sojourn in Egypt—[the Old Testament] narrative quietly makes the point that Abraham and his family inherit, in a measure, the role of Adam and Eve. . . . We could sum up this aspect of Genesis by say-

ing: Abraham's children are God's true humanity, and their homeland is the new Eden.[6]

He further quotes a Jewish rabbi who said, "God made Adam first so that if he went bad, he could send Abraham to put things right."[7]

We have referred to Abram's call. Some have suggested that a more appropriate word is "election." It is true that the call of Abram was quite different from other calls about which we read in the Old Testament, such as the call of Isaiah or Jeremiah. Moreover, the term "election" in Scripture does carry the connotation of vocation. One distinctive feature of Abram's call or election is that it was in the form of a promise. In the light of Abram's background and context, as we shall see below, one could suppose that his election would have emphasized the consequences of maintaining a certain lifestyle. However, it was the summons to neither law nor discipline. If either had been the case, he would have responded from fear rather than faith.

An important issue we need to address is the nature of Abram's election. Was it *unilateral*, as some have suggested? If so, it would have been arbitrary, because others would have been excluded. God would have been playing favorites. This is unacceptable in the light of later revelation. We must also reject the suggestion that Abram was chosen because he possessed certain inherent gifts that made him uniquely qualified for this vocation. If we do otherwise, we would be excluding the fact that the choice was by grace alone. These are important matters that have exercised the minds of theologians and biblical students from the beginning. From the Wesleyan perspective the response to them takes a specific form, but that form finds support from within the Jewish faith itself. In a video series exploring the various world religions,[8] the researcher was interviewing a Jewish rabbi and asked him the crucial question, "Why did God choose the Jews?" We ask the same question about Abram. The rabbi responded, "God was calling everyone; only Israel (Abram) heard the call and responded." The prophet Amos seconds this very Wesleyan way of answering the election question: "Are you not like the Ethiopians to me, O people of Israel? says the LORD. Did I not bring Israel up from the land of Egypt, and the Philistines from Caphtor and the Arameans from Kir?" (Amos 9:7).

Abram's election was a critical moment in human history that set in motion a movement that wove its way across the succeeding centuries through the "children of Abraham." Thus Abram became the fountainhead of a redemptive race that took many forms over the years and reached its ideal culmination in Jesus Christ and his church (composed of both Jews and Gentiles). That church became the children of Abraham in the Spirit (see Rom. 9:6-8) and so inherited the vocation of being God's redemptive agency in the world.

When Matthew, writing to a Jewish audience, began his gospel by identifying Jesus of Nazareth as the son of Abraham, he was implicitly declaring that the mediation of redemption was taking a radical new direction. And in recounting John the

Baptist's declaration that the Pharisees' claim was empty when they asserted they were children of Abraham according to the flesh (see 3:7-9), Matthew was explicitly proclaiming that the redemptive community God had all along intended was coming into being.

The old community had, by all standards, failed to fulfill its intended function. It had frustrated its election purpose by failing to understand why it had been initially chosen in Abraham. It had repeatedly failed to embody God's design for the human race in its corporate life. These failures resulted in divine judgment, culminating in the Babylonian captivity of 587 BC, which eclipsed the nation of Judah.

It is altogether possible that Matthew had this background in mind when summarizing the lineage of Jesus. The theological significance of arranging his preparatory history (1:1-17) in a sequence of fourteen generations, concluding with the Babylonian captivity, suggests what N. T. Wright has argued: from the perspective of the Jewish community at the time of Jesus' birth, the Babylonian captivity had never really ended.[9] True, some had returned home and a community of sorts had been restored under the Maccabees. However, as John Bright observed, "It was a singularly unlovely state."[10] Except for this brief period, they had never recovered the independence of the Davidic era. They had never actually been "redeemed." They never really became what they were called into being to be, a model of the kingdom of God.

Abraham himself was more than the ancestor of Israel and the spiritual ancestor of the New Israel, the church. He was (or became) a model of what God's partner in the redemptive task was to be. This claim is reflected in the extent to which a number of New Testament writers use Abraham as a pattern to be imitated. Paul uses him as an illustration of his teaching about justification by faith both in Romans (4:1-3) and Galatians (3:6-9). In both these passages Paul is referring, at least in part, to Gentile believers as children of Abraham. The author of Hebrews refers to Abraham's faith and stewardship in affirmative terms (6:13; 7:1-2; 11:8-10), and James uses Abraham's obedience to the command to sacrifice Isaac to support his argument for the importance of works as the proper expression of authentic faith (2:21-24). Peter also brings Abraham into his description of proper household relations and in doing so describes female Christians as "daughters" of Sarah (1 Pet. 3:5-6). Peter may have conveniently forgotten the Hagar incident (see below).

Abraham was not an instant saint, but he had to experience a number of "tests" to bring him to the maturity God desired him to achieve. He was a human being, finite and fallen like all of us. He did not always respond in the ideal way. But as Oswald Chambers reminds us, "The inconsistencies we find in Abraham reveal the consistency of God, and the thing to note is that Abraham remained true to God both before and after his lapses."[11] From the Genesis narratives we can conclude that by means of these tests he eventually came to the relationship described as a "friend of God" (2 Chron. 20:7; Isa. 41:8; James 2:23). The validity of this observation is reinforced by the fascinating observation of Oswald Chambers in summing up the essence of his book *The Psychology of Redemption*: "In the Life of our Lord, as Son of Man, when He transformed innocence into holiness by a series of moral choices, He gave the pattern forever of how a holy character was to be developed."[12]

His growth by way of these tests provides a series of situations that seem intended to elicit the kind of spiritual qualifications all of us, as his children in the Spirit, should desire to develop in order to be the most effective agents in the Lord's plan to redeem humankind. As we explore these tests in Abraham's pilgrimage, let us by God's grace avoid any failures he may have made and emulate the right responses that led him to the level of maturity God desires of us.

Abraham's experience reminds us that spiritual and moral growth does not occur by simply willing or wishing that it would occur. All such development takes place in the context of specific occasions in which the right responses contribute to making virtue a matter of habit. As the philosopher Aristotle said, "One swallow does not make a spring."[13] His point is that one good act or response does not create character. Rather, a lifetime of practicing the virtues is required in becoming a good person.

Two interpretive assumptions inform the following discussions. The first is the belief that Abraham and the other patriarchs (Isaac and Jacob) were real human beings. The fact that as actual human beings they were finite and fallen is the basis for Charles F. Pfeiffer's classic statement that they were "men of faith but not always faithful men."[14] On the surface, this assumption may seem obvious to the average Bible reader. However, in earlier years the existence of these men was viewed with considerable skepticism, and their stories were interpreted as mythical, the result of stories told in later times for apologetic purposes.[15] More recently, as Pfeiffer tells us, though the names of these men do not appear in nonbiblical documents, "archeological discoveries during the past half century show us that the patriarchal narratives fit in the period in which the Bible places them, and in no other. The clay tablets from Nuzi and Mari have helped us to visualize the political and the social world in which the patriarchs moved."[16] James Muilenburg reinforced Pfeiffer's conclusion: "Archeology has revealed an extraordinary correspondence between the general social and cultural conditions portrayed in Genesis and those exposed by excavations. Discoveries from such sites as Nuzi, Mari, and elsewhere, provide the geographical, cultural, linguistic, and religious background against which the stories of the patriarchs are laid."[17]

This assumption that the patriarchs were real people aids the interpretive process in two ways. First, it enables us to legitimately use a measure of imagination to suggest realistic human responses and attitudes beyond what the text actually says.[18] Second, it enables us to evaluate the setting of Abraham's life and behavior more adequately by knowing his historical context.

The second interpretive assumption takes into account the structure of biblical theology that informs the entire Bible. Broader in scope than the study of a single text, this assumption allows us to interpret the experiences of Abraham theologically within this larger context. This assumption is what informs the opening discussion of this introduction and explains the point of view from which these devotional studies proceed. This assumption is also the basis for treating the biblical text as we have it. Many critical scholars fragment the text by identifying different sources that have been merged to produce the present form of the narrative. Even if these analyses are in some measure credible, the final form of the material is still informed by the central theological thread that gives unity to the story of God.[19]

There is an additional theological assumption that is relevant to contemporary religious experience. Genesis 15:6 plainly asserts that by his faith in the promise of God, Abram was declared righteous—that is, justified in status. This is the meaning of "righteousness" as used in that verse. Both terms—"righteous" and "justified"—translate the same Hebrew word group. This will be explored more fully as we proceed. But for our purposes here the term "righteous" (or "righteousness"), when understood correctly, does not imply anything about moral character or virtue. That means that Abram was brought into a right relation with God by grace alone, apart from any kind of moral worthiness. But on the basis of that status, he was called to develop the kind of moral character consistent with his vocation as God's redemptive agent. It is this moral development in Abram's life that we are exploring in these studies. The order of experience in Abram's life is precisely the pattern that appears when we attempt to understand the biblical relation between justification and sanctification.[20] As John Wesley insisted, sanctification begins with justification, although he insists that the two should not be confused, since justification is a *relative* change while sanctification is a *real* change. For the New Testament believer, justification is understood as the beginning of a process of increasing conformity to the "mind of Christ." This process will continue throughout life and beyond and, as Wesley put it, is "faith working by love." Thus the aspect of Abram's development explored here really provides us some insights into the developing life of holiness in the justified Christian believer.

However, we need to include one caution. The theme of Abraham's testing is not new but is found in rabbinic teaching. His tests or trials are usually considered in the Talmud as being ten in number, although there is no precise agreement on what they were. However, for our purposes, what is important is that they are always considered meritorious both for Abraham and his posterity.[21] We must reject this interpretation of Abraham's tests because it would invalidate the biblical teaching about his justification by faith and distort the New Testament teaching about sanctification. So rather than the attainment of merit, the tests result in the development of character. Keeping these details in mind throws some interesting light on John the Baptist's accusation of the Pharisees' dependence on their descent from Abraham as a basis for divine acceptance.

In summary, the purpose in these studies is twofold: devotional and theological. These two emphases are related, since a sound devotional life is, or should be, informed by sound, scripturally based theology. The perceptive reader will recognize that the author has derived some tremendous spiritual insights from Oswald Chambers' small book on Abraham, a work he discovered well into the development of this project and which for him has provided many scintillating pinpoints of light. Theologically, the relation of Abraham to God has numerous important theological implications that open the door to discussions of issues that reflect the Wesleyan theological perspective. These studies have thus drawn from John Wesley's analysis of the divine-human relationship several insights that throw light on the spiritual life.

ONE

The Test of Discipleship

GEN. 11:27—12:3

As far as Scripture is concerned, our knowledge of Abram before his initial encounter with the Lord is restricted to a family tree spelled out in some detail at the conclusion of Gen. 11. We learn that compared to twenty-first-century standards, his immediate ancestors lived long lives, so he evidently had sturdy genes. Abram's immediate family first lived in Ur of the Chaldeans, making him a native of the ancient area known as Mesopotamia. He was one of three brothers, each of which had a wife. Abram's wife was named Sarai, and evidently the biblical writer was laying a foundation for subsequent marvelous divine actions in the life of this couple by mentioning that Sarai was barren, which was perceived in the ancient world as a curse for women.

This early record in Scripture gives us no clue as to the religious life of Abram's family. However, we can make a reasonable inference from ancient records of religious practices in the

Mesopotamian area. References to Babylonian life in texts such as Isa. 8:19 suggest that occult practices were widespread and no doubt included worship of astral deities. Joshua 24:15 implies that Abram's family members were idolaters as well.

Donald J. Wiseman describes the religious situation in Ur based on ancient documents:

> Religion in Babylonia at this time was polytheism of the grossest type. . . . more than three hundred distinct gods were worshipped. . . . Small idols, images and figurines (possibly the *teraphim* mentioned in Genesis xxxi. 19) were manufactured from clay by potters near the temple area. According to Jewish tradition Abraham's father traded in these idols and this polytheism was a feature of Abraham's early home life from which he revolted. His father is said to have worshipped twelve different gods. . . . "Your fathers dwelt of old beyond the river (Euphrates), Terah, the father of Abraham, and the father of Nahor; and they served other gods" (Joshua xxiv. 2).[1]

Thus is it reasonably clear that Abram, along with his ancestors, was an idolater before God graciously revealed himself to him. This does not mean that Abram rejected all his former practices when he began to follow the "voice." As Abram followed the Lord, we will see both a growing faith and a developing ethical maturity. This transition from idolatry to ethical maturity did not occur quickly, simply, or easily. Contemporary Christians nurtured from childhood in the church may find it difficult to be patient with new converts to Christ who do not immediately reflect model Christian behavior. Judged by the ideals embodied in God's creative intention for the human race, many, like Abram, fall miserably short. One of the most notable examples is John Newton, celebrated author of the popular hymn "Amazing Grace." For some time following his dramatic conversion from the depths of sin and corruption he remained the captain of a slave-trading ship, having, as he said, "sweet communion with the Lord." But as he matured, he realized the inconsistency of this occupation with being a Christian.

The idolatry of the heavenly bodies is probably reflected in a Jewish legend that when Abram started on his journeys, he saw the stars in the heavens and said, "I will worship the stars." But when the stars set, Abram saw the constellations, such as the Pleiades, and said, "I will worship the constellations." But the constellations also set. Then Abram saw the moon sailing high in the heavens and said, "I will worship the moon." But the moon also vanished when her season was over. Then Abram saw the sun in all his majesty, coming out of his chamber like a bridegroom and rejoicing as a strong runner in a race. But when the day was spent, he saw the sun sink on the western horizon. Stars, constellations, moon, sun—all were unworthy of his worship, for all had set and disappeared. Then Abram said, "I will worship God, for He abides forever."

Knowing all this we are left with the impression that there was little in Abram's background that would have prepared him for an encounter with the true and living God, except what Wesleyans would call prevenient grace. But God's grace is always a mystery. It does not conform to human standards or plans. It may appear without cause—except for the mercy of God—and without normal human preparation. But whether or not we can explain it, what is most important is that this pagan man heard and responded to the "voice."

Although these studies mainly focus on one aspect of the Abraham saga, we will give some attention here to another that is also important. This other aspect is suggested by the preceding observation about Abram's awareness of a "voice" that transcended his culture and by the words of E. A. Speiser: "Abraham's journey to the Promised Land was thus no routine expedition of several hundred miles. Instead, it was the start of an epic voyage in search of spiritual truths, a quest that was to constitute the central theme of all biblical history."[2]

Because he followed the "voice," Abram was always on the move. By living this way in the Promised Land Abram developed an understanding of God that distinguished God from contemporary objects of worship. In that period—and later as well—the prevailing polytheistic religion was characterized by numerous local gods. Thus each local area had its own god who was limited to that place. The idea that Abram's God was mobile—not restricted to one city or place, but equally present wherever Abram camped—was a significant theological development. As A. Carter Shelley says, "A mobile God was one of the primary contributions made by the Hebrews."[3] In the light of the numerous worship shrines dedicated to Baal in Canaan, and soon taken over by the Israelites, this concept of God was probably the basis for the Shema, found in Deut. 6:4-5: "Hear, O Israel: The LORD is our God, the LORD alone."

Contemporary readers of the Bible may have a difficult time grasping the radical nature of the call of Abram. With centuries of theological development and biblical knowledge about the Lord available to them, people today often fail to realize that Abram of Ur was not privy to any of this information. All Abram had to go on was a "voice." As he followed that "voice," we find Abram not only maturing ethically in his own character but also increasingly understanding the character of the One whose "voice" he had heard.[4] Thus an important part of his journey, which possibly takes on new elements at each stage, is a growing knowledge of the One whom he named El, the name of the Semitic high god that was often associated with other descriptive terms (e.g., El Shaddai [God Almighty]). It was only at the revelation of the divine name at the burning bush that the children of Abraham came to know the One they called El as Yahweh (Exod. 6:2-4).[5]

This way of thinking about Abraham's theological development is suggested by the observations of Pfeiffer:

There are few if any practices in Abraham's worship that are unique, except the object of that worship. Far more important are the elements that are missing, specifically the preoccupation with fertility and ceremonies connected with the yearly agricultural cycle. . . . The truly unique element of Abraham's faith was the special place that he had in the purposes of God and his obedience in fulfilling those purposes.[6]

However we may explain the call, when it came, it was a call for Abram to turn his back on his past and step out into an unknown future. In a sense, that is always the nature of the divine call. The future is unknown to us, and only God knows the implications of our present decisions. Because of the environment in which Abram was immersed, we can say that responding to God's voice meant dropping a curtain on the past. This was a decision that meant more than physical separation from his family, his home environment, and the familiar setting that had up till now shaped his life. It meant a separation involving his values, priorities, and worldview. The latter would be the most difficult separation and would take time and maturation. Oswald Chambers describes the difficulty of this separation in these words: "One of the hardest lessons to learn is the one brought out by Abraham's obedience to the call of God. He went 'out' of all his own ways of looking at things and became a fool in the eyes of the world."[7]

Based on the call of Abram in Gen. 12:1 that is marked by an increasingly personal identification ("from your country and your kindred and your father's house"), Jewish scholar N. Liebowitz points out that this sequence is contrary to what would be expected, for the logical sequence is that one first leaves his home, then his birthplace, and after that his country. She concurs with early Jewish commentators that what is being suggested by the passage is "a spiritual rather than physical withdrawal, beginning with the periphery and ending with the inner core."[8]

We have a reasonable sense of what Abram's call was *from* and, from our contemporary perspective, what it was *to*, but from Abram's point of view, it was a total mystery. It was a call into a relationship with God "for his own purposes, and the test of faith is to believe that God knows what he is after. The call of God only becomes clear as we obey, never as we weigh the *pros* and *cons* and try to reason it out."[9]

The narrative tells us that Abram was seventy-five years old at the time of his departure from Haran. It is true that he was not an old man by contemporary standards, but he was no "spring chicken." He could easily have reasoned that at this age, it made no sense to leave the comforts and securities he enjoyed, abandon an urban area of advanced civilization and wealth, and head out into the barren land to the west.

The difficulty of Abram's response may be seen by his not pulling up stakes until his father, Terah, had died. His initial call came while his family was living in Ur of the Chaldeans. For whatever reason, the family's relocation at Haran to the north began with the intention to go to Canaan, but Terah decided to remain there.[10] It was here that God apparently spoke the second time to Abram, calling him to go farther, and it was from this point that his pilgrimage began. All calls to discipleship are calls to go farther.

What do we make of this? It is reasonably easy to explain from a human point of view. Abram lived within a patriarchal culture that had strict mores about family life. The oldest male in the extended family was considered the patriarch and his was the role of absolute ruler of the family, making decisions that were binding for every member of the clan. The patriarch served as the priest, judge, and arbiter of all relations including marriage. Thus if a young member of the family declared his independence and left the oversight of the patriarch, that young person was viewed in a strongly negative way.[11] We see this acted out later in the case of Esau. This strong cultural influence was possibly the reason for Abram's delay in responding to the voice he heard. When Terah—his father and patriarch—died, the door was open for him to make the decision to leave home and country and head into the unknown.

Nevertheless, this was a traumatic decision that meant making a clean break with the past. The author remembers the response his own family made in becoming Christians. There was a trip to a prayer altar, followed by actions that symbolized leaving the old life behind. A bonfire was kindled—in the heating stove—and family members burned everything in the house they associated with the past. No doubt some of the items burned represented innocent practices, but the action signified a commitment to live out the grace they had experienced.

This kind of initial response has ongoing consequences, and decisions must be made along the way. Rare is the person who does not stumble at some point in pursuing that course. Abram, too, had some failures along the way, but there is no indication that he ever looked back. Dr. A. K. Bracken would often say to his students, "No matter how often I stumble and fall, I will always get up with my face toward the city of God."

The children of Abraham are called to the same response. Jesus' call to discipleship demanded the same radical reply:

> Whoever comes to me and does not hate father and mother, wife and children, brothers and sisters, yes, and even life itself, cannot be my disciple. Whoever does not carry the cross and follow me cannot be my disciple. For which of you, intending to build a tower, does not first sit down and estimate the cost, to see whether he has enough to complete it? Otherwise, when he has laid a foundation and is not able to finish, all who see it will begin to ridicule him, saying, "This fellow began to build, and was not able to finish." . . . So therefore, none of you can become my disciple if you do not give up all your possessions. (Luke 14:25-30, 33)

Like Abram, this response has both a negative and a positive side. It means leaving behind the old way of life. Like Matthew, who left behind the "tax booth" (Matt. 9:9), and Peter and John, who left behind their fishing nets (4:18-22), the Lord calls us to "burn the bridges behind us." On the positive side, we are called to a new relationship, to become part of a new family to which we are to give our primary loyalty, the family of Abraham, the friend of God.

TWO

The Test of Integrity
GEN. 12:10-20

We have now examined the call Abram received from God, its radical nature, and the way he responded to it by turning his back on family, culture, religion, and country to follow it. We noted that he was about seventy-five years of age, not really a young man. No wonder he has been called the pioneer of faith. Yet the most profound act of commitment is a life lived moment by moment in faith and dedication. The next event the Bible records about Abram happened soon after his arrival in the Promised Land. It is the story of how he failed a test of courage, which was also a test of integrity. Although the situation was very embarrassing to Abram, he no doubt learned a significant lesson from it. This incident clearly demonstrates that Abram was no "plaster saint." This is true of most of the major biblical characters. They were real people just like us, and the Bible does not hesitate to speak of their failures.

All biblical characters—except One—manifest inconsistencies. When we study their lives, we are not looking for perfect human examples but the faithfulness of God to his people through all their stumblings and shortcomings. This reality does not mean we celebrate our failures as if we were proud of them. Rather we should celebrate God's grace and what he is able to accomplish in our finite lives and learn from our shortcomings.

Often people in the ancient Near East would migrate from place to place in order to find food. In Abram's case, a drought caused food to become scarce in Canaan, so he headed for Egypt. Here we get the first clue that Sarai was a beautiful woman—despite her seemingly advanced age. Knowing that the men of Egypt would be attracted to his wife, Abraham believed they would dispose of him to gain access to her. Thus he instructed her to lie about their relationship. It was not actually a total lie, since she was his half sister, but his intention was to deceive and that is really the purpose of a lie, a purpose that can be accomplished without saying a word.

Where did Abram go astray? Unfortunately he was occupied with what was happening around him instead of with the promise of God. God had called him to leave his country and go to a land he would show him, which turned out to be the land of Canaan. The call was accompanied by a promise of blessing—and protection. Thus his decision to go to Egypt and protect himself through deception was a failure of faith. As a matter of fact, every failure in the religious life is a failure of faith.

There is no indication that Abram sought God's guidance in his decision to go down to Egypt. It seemed the most natural thing to do, so apparently he just made the decision based on common sense. As W. H. Griffith Thomas said, "It would certainly seem that Abraham was now thinking solely of the land and its famine, and forgetting God and his promises."[1] This response shows how easy it is to get our eyes on circumstances and forget the faithfulness of God to his pledged word. But as Thomas added, "Difficulties do not necessarily indicate that we are out of the pathway of God's will."[2]

The real tragedy in this act of deception was that Abram was concerned only for his own safety; he had no apparent thought for Sarai's well-being. Notice the personal pronouns ("me," "my") in Gen. 12:13. He probably excused himself because he was only asking Sarai to support a half-truth (cf. 20:13). Moreover, since she was a female and culturally less valuable than a male, Sarai had to be fully submissive to her husband. For all practical purposes, as A. Carter Shelley put it, "In the crudest terms, Abram pimps Sarai."[3] There are many more problems here, but most importantly, taking into account that both male and female are created in the image of God, what Abram did is less than moral. Philosopher Immanuel Kant captured the Christian perspective on the treatment of others in his categorical imperative: "Treat all persons, including yourself, as an end and never merely as a means." That is, personhood is of great value and should never be treated as an "it" to be disposed of at will. In a word, people should never use other people for their own selfish ends. This is a great principle to live by and clearly reflects the exalted value of personhood, whatever the gender, as held by Jesus.

A further disaster resulting from Abram's actions was the creation of an uncertain future. Even if Pharaoh never consummated his marriage with Sarai, just making her his "wife" jeopardized the fulfillment of God's promise to Abram, at least with Sarai. The man to whom God had promised children now had no wife with whom to have them. In the words of von Rad, "What concerns us most is the betrayal of the ancestress, and one must not exactly restrain one's thought if they recognize in the bearer of the promise himself the greatest enemy of the promise; for its greatest threat comes from him."[4]

Another great tragedy related to the purpose for which Abram was elected also occurred. He damaged the possibility of influencing others positively for his God. No doubt Abram had to slink out of Egypt with his tail between his legs, deeply humiliated by the less-than-admirable way the pagans on the Nile thought of the moral standards of his religion.

Oswald Chambers made the astute observation that "whenever [Abram] neglected to erect an altar, he went astray,"[5] and we read of no altar or prayer in Egypt. But to Abram's credit, he did some things right. When the situation came to light and he had been reprimanded by Pharaoh for his deception, there is no evidence that he attempted to justify himself.[6] And when he returned to his rightful place in Canaan, he returned to the altar he had previously built (see 13:4).

What did Abram learn from this test? He should have learned at least four things. First, there is the lesson of truth. The child of God is to be honest in all attitudes and avoid all deception in actions. The end does not justify the means. This applies to a person's moral life, church work, social status, and family life, as well as personal ambition. Not only must the end we seek be true, but the means we use must also be true.

Second, Abram should have learned that God was essential to his every step and that nothing can be done without him. As Jesus said, in his analogy of the vine and the branches, "Apart from me you can do nothing" (John 15:5). Walter Brueggemann observes that this incident in Abram's life, as well as other failures, "guards against any inclination to interpret Abraham's faith as having been easy or without anguish."[7]

Another lesson Abram should have learned was that it was unwise to trust his own shrewdness. Further, he should have learned that God was able, in spite of the famine, to provide for him and his family in the place God intended them to be.

Even though Abram was not faithful, he found that God was faithful. God had not forgotten his promises to his servant. Thus Abram evidently came away with a deeper understanding of God and a louder call for a simple, absolute, continual trust. And with his return to Canaan, to the altar he left, he learned that God can always be found where we leave him. The hymn writer William H. Bathurst expressed the right attitude toward the pressure to lose faith:

> *O for a faith that will not shrink,*
> > *Tho' pressed by ev'ry foe,*
> *That will not tremble on the brink*
> > *Of any earthly woe!*
>
> . . . .
>
> *A faith that shines more bright and clear*
> > *When tempests rage without;*
> *That when in danger knows no fear,*
> > *In darkness feels no doubt.*[8]

In the ill-fated trip to Egypt we are looking at Abram, but the narrator makes us aware that God's promise is not dependent on Abram's faithfulness. What matters is the faithfulness of Yahweh to his pledged word. It would be incorrect to suggest that this truth implies that an individual's relationship with God continues regardless of his or her faith or behavior. God's faithfulness in this case refers to his choice of a family whose members will be the agents of redemptive blessing to a lost creation. Although they will undergo significant transformation throughout their subsequent history, these agents of that purpose will culminate in the one "seed of Abraham" becoming the one faithful Israelite. Thus the promise will come to consummation, just as it also will in the face of the failures and foibles of the church, whose members ideally should be the children of Abraham.

Unfortunately, Abram apparently had an inordinate fear for his own safety and he relapsed into the same failure later on in another situation, with similar results (Gen. 20:1-18). Some critical scholars suggest that both stories are of the same event. Furthermore, Isaac is reported to have fallen into the same sin (see 26:6-11). However this is interpreted, it does suggest the family had a personality flaw that made more than one appearance. Like most such weaknesses, this flaw would need a period of discipline for internal change to occur. There are some important practical implications here for each of us as we honestly look at ourselves in the light of what it means to be truly Christlike.

THREE

The Test of Self-Interest
GEN. 13:1-11; PHIL. 2:5-16

Following Abram's failure in Egypt and his return to the altar where he had first worshipped the Lord in the Land of Promise, he evidently began to recover the faith that had prompted his initial response to be God's pioneer. He had become exceedingly wealthy, though that does not imply that faithfulness to God will bring us wealth. Actually, much of his wealth resulted from his failure to be faithful to God's promise. Moreover, this wealth, in the form of livestock, became the occasion for strife within his family. It was Abram's response to this dissension that displayed his developing trust in God. Gerhard von Rad observes that this is "one of the few passages in the patriarchal history where the figure of the patriarch is also intended by the narrator to be exemplary. The contrast which this picture of Abraham makes with that of the previous story is great."[1]

For the sake of peace, Abram did not insist on his rights. Since there was no law except the customs generally accepted in the patriarchal culture, Abram's rights were not legal but moral. Yet they were rights nevertheless, and he would be justified in claiming them. As the head of the clan, the patriarch had the authority to determine the activities of each member, and Lot was a subordinate member of the extended family. Abram thus had the right to say to him, "You go and find a place for your cattle wherever you can. I will retain access to the rich pastureland around us in this location." But he did not do that. From a religious perspective, the right to the land was his by virtue of the divine promise. He could claim a "divine right" to pasture his flocks wherever he chose. This has often been the sanction that some people have used to gain their own ends and take advantage of others. But Abram did not do that.

In refusing to insist on his rights he anticipated the attitude of Jesus that Paul describes in Phil. 2:5-6: "Think of yourselves the way Christ Jesus thought of himself. He had equal status with God but didn't think so much of himself that he had to cling to the advantages of that status no matter what" (TM).[2]

This attitude and response is the opposite of what classic Christian thought has identified as egocentricity, the sinful attitude that asserts one's rights over those of others and exalts oneself even above God. This attitude is the essence of sinfulness, and Abram showed that he was growing beyond it.

Abram's faith displayed in his generosity toward Lot demonstrated his recognition that what he was to inherit was a gift. He would not receive it through manipulation or by asserting his rights; he would instead receive it through faith by allowing God to provide it in his own time and way. This suggests that Abram was coming to understand a concept of reality different from the common herd. Similarly, the children of Abraham are called to be "heirs, not predators, purchasers, or thieves."³

One of the sad consequences of the strife is suggested by Gen. 13:7: "The Canaanites and Perizzites lived in the land." While this may simply be a historical statement, it has significant implications. These two groups must have seen and overheard the quarrels between the servants of God's children. What kind of influence would that have had? Would Abram's mission to be a pattern of God's design for human relations have been appropriately modeled? Consider Paul's words in Phil. 2:14-16: "Do all things without murmurings and arguing, so that you may be blameless and innocent, children of God without blemish in the midst of a crooked and perverse generation, in which you shine like stars in the world."

One pastor made a sad confession:

For years, I played on one of the church's softball teams in a league made up entirely of church-sponsored teams from the area. I was always a defensive liability. I was there mostly as comic relief, and each game the team had to decide where to put me so that I would not ruin our chances. Frequently, therefore, I was the catcher, and because of this I began to know some of the umpires from the local association of professional umpires. I will never forget what one umpire said after a brutal game in which he was vilified and the teams were at swords' points. As he walked off the field, he said, "There is nothing I hate more than umpiring church leagues. There is less joy, less honesty, and less good will in these games than anywhere else." I was embarrassed for myself and for everyone else on the field because this presumably non-Christian umpire wanted nothing to do with the churches he saw represented in front of him.[4]

This is quite a contrast to the relationship between John Wesley and George Whitefield. They were on opposite teams theologically, but personally there was a relationship that demonstrated the Spirit of Christ. Their differences never manifested themselves in harsh words or broken communion. When Whitefield died, Wesley preached his funeral.

This incident in the lives of Abram and his nephew Lot presents us with several contrasts that highlight the importance of cultivating the right spirit and attitude in being the true children of Abraham. For example, note the contrast between Abram's response to the situation here and the self-centeredness he manifested in the visit to Egypt.

Note also the contrast between Abram and Lot. The point at issue was the value system on which each based his decision. Lot's choice was founded on what could be called worldliness.

John White, in his book *The Golden Cow*, speaks of the effects of worldliness on believers:

> It comes to this: we Christians are too often like sponges soaked to capacity with the value system of the society we live in. Whether we sympathize with labor or industry, whether we are Republicans, Democrats, conservatives, liberals, socialists, or whatever, our value systems in practice are one. We may argue fiercely with one another, but we base our arguments on the same premise: the greatest good in life is a bigger (or better cooked) slice of this world's pie, a pie to which we all have an inalienable right.[5]

Lot's decision was motivated by self-interest, without regard for Abram and his rights or best interest. His decision was calculated to obtain what he wanted when he wanted it; it was based on what he saw before him that reminded him of Egypt. That his appetite had been influenced by the time spent in Egypt may be suggested by Gen. 13:10: "Lot looked about him, and saw that the plain of the Jordan was well watered everywhere like the garden of the LORD, like the land of Egypt, in the direction of Zoar."

By contrast, Abram's decision was based on faith in the promises of God and on the future in the light of those promises. Long before Jesus announced the principle, Abram embodied it: "Blessed are the meek, for they will inherit the earth" (Matt. 5:5). Based on his confidence in the promises of God, Abram believed he would eventually inherit the land. While the

Promised Land in the Old Testament was enclosed within the limits of a narrow strip of real estate along the Mediterranean Sea, those limits disappear in the New Testament age of fulfillment. On this matter N. T. Wright points out that "as Paul insists, in line with some other Jewish thinkers of the time, the promises to Abraham were that he should inherit, not just one small strip of territory, but the whole world (Romans 4:13)."[6] This transformation invalidates the teaching that makes Israel's possession of the limited piece of land in the Middle East essential to God's future for the children of Abraham.

Finally, notice the consequences of the respective decisions. The outcome for Lot is hinted at in Gen. 13:13: "Now the people of Sodom were wicked, great sinners against the LORD." The devastating result is reported later. The consequence for Abram is reported in verses 14-18:

> The LORD said to Abram, after Lot had separated from him, "Raise your eyes now, and look from the place where you are, northward and southward and eastward and westward; for all the land that you see I will give to you and to your offspring forever. I will make your offspring like the dust of the earth; so that if one can count the dust of the earth, your offspring also can be counted. Rise up, walk through the length and the breadth of the land, for I will give it to you." So Abram moved his tent, and came and settled by the oaks of Mamre, which are at Hebron; and there he built an altar to the LORD.

One further challenge to Abram's faith possibly attends the departure of Lot to the cities of the plain, which lay outside the land of Canaan. The promise of an heir was as yet unfulfilled. While possession of the land appears in the forefront of this particular story, the ongoing saga of the problem of an heir ties the entire story of Abram/Abraham together. Larry R. Helyer argues that Lot's departure introduces a crisis to the problem, since "Abram's heir-apparent virtually eliminates himself from the promise by leaving the land of promise, Canaan. Now Abram is without any heir."[7]

FOUR

The Test of Forgiveness

GEN. 14:14-16

No sooner had Abram settled down to a peaceful life after the conflict over grazing land, than an emergency arose, presenting him with a new experience and a new challenge to his faith. On learning that Lot had been taken prisoner by the kings invading Sodom and Gomorrah, he was faced with a decision. He could have said, "It serves him right" or "He got just what was coming to him." After all, Lot had taken advantage of his uncle's generosity and left Abram to forage on the least desirable pasture. But Abram revealed that he was making headway in becoming the model of what God's redemptive agent in the world should be. As Gen. 14:14 says, "When Abram heard that his nephew had been taken captive," he did not hesitate but took action.

There is a negative and a positive side to forgiveness. If Abram had decided to ignore the plight of Lot, his choice would likely have had a negative effect on his own spirit. Even medical authorities recognize that harboring grudges or resentments causes a canker in the soul. In a word, forgiveness is important for both physical and psychological well-being, to say nothing of spiritual health. Although there is no direct evidence in the text concerning Abram's feelings, his immediate response to the matter makes it clear that he was not holding a grudge.

It is interesting that the Old Testament does not include any reference to forgiving one's neighbor. There are many references to God's forgiveness of human sin. In fact, the refusal to forgive and the desire for vengeance are attitudes frequently expressed in the Psalms, and the main message of the book of Obadiah reeks with the desire for revenge. In the light of these matters, Abram's response seems unusual and reflects an attitude that becomes most explicit in the New Testament, where forgiveness of others is essential to receiving divine forgiveness. It could be argued that such forgiveness is the logical implication of the command in Leviticus to "love your neighbor as yourself" (19:18) and that there are several examples of forgiveness throughout the Old Testament. Joseph, in the light of the providence of God, forgave his brothers (Gen. 50:15-21). David, contrary to common practice, apparently forgave Jonathan's son, Mephibosheth, giving him a place at the royal table (2 Sam. 9).

What about Lot? He had been delivered from slavery and his goods restored thanks to Abram's intervention. What was his response? If we could know how he responded, it might throw additional light on the nature of forgiveness, but little is said. He apparently returned to his dwelling in Sodom to continue his involvement in the life of that city. We have no indication from the text that he manifested any gratitude toward Abram. Perhaps he even assumed that he deserved the blessing he experienced. While we are not primarily concerned with Lot, if his response to Abram's gracious action on his behalf is as suggested here, it tells us that forgiveness does not necessarily entail a transformation of either behavior or attitude on the part of the one forgiven. Forgiveness is an attitude of the forgiver, and if the relationship is not restored with the "forgivee," the forgiver is still benefited by relinquishing his or her self-destructive attitudes.

Again, we are not given any clue to Abram's response, except perhaps in his reaction to the king of Sodom's offer of a huge reward (see Gen. 14:21-24). However, we can legitimately conclude that Abram displayed a generous spirit that transcended the normal response of fallen human beings. His response was also godlike, since from the beginning of human history to Abram's time, God had demonstrated his intention to restore relations with his fallen creation through forgiveness. This intention would be fully displayed in the gift of his Son, the "seed of Abraham," who would offer forgiveness to "the lost, the last, and the least."[1] By dying on the cross, Christ vividly demonstrated the divine willingness to forgive. On this basis, Paul observed that among the ethical virtues for the new life in Christ, believers should "be kind to one another, tenderhearted, forgiving one another, as God in Christ has forgiven you" (Eph. 4:32).

FIVE

The Test of Faith, Part 1

GEN. 15:1-6

As we have observed, every test Abram faced was a test of faith, but the events recorded in Gen. 15 are especially centered on that aspect of his life with God. Because of the significance of this issue, Gen. 15 deserves special attention. It is one of the most important chapters in the Bible for understanding our relationship with God. As Walter Brueggemann said about verse 6, "No other Old Testament text has exercised such a compelling influence on the New Testament."[1] Genesis 15 is divided into two parts, and in both Abram is seeking some assurance that God is going to keep his word. God has made promises to Abram, but so far in the narrative, there has been no evidence of their fulfillment.

Many believers have a faulty idea of faith, and Abram's faith provides a clear model for a proper understanding. Faith is not, as many suppose, a self-generated desire for certain things to happen. Rather, faith is a believing response to a divine promise (see Rom. 10:17), and Abram had received certain promises on which his faith was based. It was not wishful thinking. What is significant for our purposes is the implication of the story that these promises were so conditioned at the outset that they would, in the course of time, put Abram's faith to the test. On the very threshold of the promise of a son, the writer declared, "Now Sarai was barren; she had no child" (Gen. 11:30).

The theme of barrenness runs like a dark thread throughout the Abraham-Sarah narratives, from beginning to near end, when Isaac is finally born. Walter Brueggemann describes the theme as "an effective metaphor for hopelessness. There is no foreseeable future. There is no human power to invent a future."[2] Its mention at the very threshold of redemptive history (12:1-3) is a comment about the condition of the human race after the unsuccessful attempt at self-salvation in the Tower of Babel incident. All such efforts likewise lead to dead ends; they fail miserably at addressing the deepest need of humankind.

That God speaks a word of promise in the midst of hopelessness and eventually brings about a solution is evidence of what God can do. Only he can speak an answer that leads out of barrenness and into a meaningful and viable future. The divine initiative is emphasized at the outset as God repeatedly declares, "I will . . ." Here God declares his intention to bring about a future that Abram and Sarai cannot produce on their own. Here is the call for faith.

It is no coincidence that the theme of barrenness appears again and again throughout the history of Abram's family. Rebekah (25:21) and Rachel (29:31), both playing major roles in continuing Abram's redemptive lineage, are barren until God intervenes. At an unusually low point in the history of the people of Israel, as described in the book of Judges, the theme recurs with Hannah (1 Sam. 1—2). In this case, Hannah's barrenness is no doubt symbolic of the inability of mere human resources to bring about God's promise of a land. Once again, God intervenes, removes the barrenness, and sends Samuel, whose integrity and wisdom bring about a temporary solution.

The theme continues in the midst of the Babylonian captivity of 587 BC. When the future seems lost for the nation of Judah, Isaiah appropriates the theme and announces God's intervention: "Sing, O barren one who did not bear; burst into song and shout, you who have not been in labor! For the children of the desolate woman will be more than the children of her that is married, says the LORD" (Isa. 54:1). But by the time Augustus is emperor of Rome and Herod the Great is king of Judea the barrenness persists. The exile has not ended, the people of God are still subject to foreign powers, and the deliverance repeatedly promised has not materialized. In the midst of this seeming hopelessness God once again opens the womb of a barren woman (Elizabeth) and brings about the pregnancy of a young virgin (Mary). Then the death and resurrection of the virgin's Son, the "seed of Abraham," brings an end to the barrenness and opens the door to hope for the human race. In Jesus of Nazareth the emptiness finally can be filled, the slavery broken, and the future transformed into hope, for those who have faith in him.

So in keeping with this theme, as soon as Abram and his extended family entered the Promised Land, the narrator declares, "At that time the Canaanites were in the land" (Gen. 12:6*b*). He had found the land, camped in various places throughout it, but it was clearly not in his possession. Others occupied it and owned it; how was he to acquire it? What kind of miracle was the Lord going to perform to bring his word to pass? The stage was set with challenges to God's promises and thus the testing of Abram's faith. In this chapter we find Abram questioning the promises.

It is significant that Abram questions God at this point. Genesis 15 opens with the words, "After these things . . ." (v. 1). What "things"? Abram had just experienced a great victory in battle. He had vanquished a superior force and consummated the victory with an act of generosity. Drawing on the study of Jewish scholar Nahum Sarna, Helyer observes that "by his bold intervention and rescue of Lot, Abram exposes himself to the endemic plague of that region—wars of retaliation."[3] It is altogether likely that, like Elijah after the contest with the prophets of Baal on Mount Carmel, Abram was undergoing a bout of depression, what someone has called "the valley of the afterward." The human spirit is not a machine, and high emotional moments can sometimes produce emotional lows. Many things can have this effect, and a failure to recognize this fact can destabilize a person's faith. This is a natural human response. Many a preacher has delivered a rousing sermon, sprinkling stardust on the congregation, and then experienced a sharp sense of despondency afterward. Even God seemed to recognize the letdown in Abram's spirit and sought to shore it up with the comforting words, "Do not be afraid, Abram, I am your shield" (v. 1).

But Abram's words here do indeed reflect a deep sense of despondency, disappointment, or discouragement: "O Lord God, what will you give me, for I continue childless, and the heir of my house is Eliezer of Damascus?" (v. 3). What we are seeing in Abram confirms he was a normal human being experiencing a natural human response. As Oswald Chambers observed, "A saint is not an angel and never will be; a saint is the flesh and blood theatre in which the decrees of God are carried to successful issue."[4]

To God's attempt to bolster Abram's faith by declaring himself to be Abram's shield, Abram in effect responded, "O Lord God, what's the purpose of your gifts, when I'm still childless?" Abram is not rebellious, but he is not feeling particularly blessed either. His words are not a challenge to God but an expression of resignation; perhaps he is even blaming himself for misinterpreting God. At this time he is about ninety-five years old; twenty years have passed since he "thought" he received the promise. Abram's wagon is stuck in the mud, but God is pointing him to the stars and is suggesting he hitch his wagon to them.

As numerous interpreters have commented on this encounter, "God's delays are not denials." We may infer that the delay was intended to bring Abram nearer to God and to lead him to depend more on the Giver than on his gifts. So in the face of unexplained delay Abram's faith shook off its doubts "and he believed the LORD" (v. 6).

What did Abram believe? He heard nothing new; he saw no marvelous manifestation of power. Brueggemann addresses this question in an insightful way: "Surely it is not because he feels new generative power in his loins. Nor because he has new expectations for Sarah. The new promise for his life is not any expectation of flesh and blood. Rather, he has come to rely on the promise speaker. He has now permitted God to be not a hypothesis about the future, but the voice around which his life is organized."[5]

Abram's believing on this occasion became the basis for Paul identifying New Testament believers (both Jew and Gentile) as children of Abraham. As a result of Abram's faith, God "reckoned it to him as righteousness" (v. 6; see Rom. 4:22). In fact, this part of the passage lays the foundation for one of the major theological teachings of the Bible.

The Hebrew term translated "righteousness" is *tsedaqah*, which is the same word translated as "justification," the term used by both Jesus and Paul to refer to God's declaration that one has been "put right." The history of Christian thought reflects the struggle of God's people to understand the meaning of this concept. That struggle is between two ideas of what righteousness means, or how it is acquired, and thus how to be acceptable to God. One way is to become righteous by keeping the law, while the other, the way God intended, is to be declared righteous by faith.

This is the struggle the apostle Paul had in his own experience and in attempting to identify the uniqueness of the Christian faith in relation to Judaism. Oddly enough, by failing to recognize the meaning of righteousness in this context, influential teachers throughout most of Christian history have taught that we are justified by the righteousness acquired through the Law. Following the teaching of Augustine that justification means to "make righteous," the church came to believe that the ethical righteousness by which God accepts us is acquired by good works. Certain activities, such as pilgrimages and other religious rites, acquired merit. Surplus merit acquired by others, including Jesus, could be appropriated—or bought—to assure one's own salvation or to hasten the passage of a loved one through purgatory.

This way of earning God's favor was the setting in which Martin Luther experienced the frustration of failure that led him eventually to discover another meaning of righteousness. From his biblical studies he found that instead of referring to righteousness as God's requirement, Paul was speaking in Romans about righteousness being God's mercy for the helpless. The righteousness referred to is thus God's own. This set Luther free from the bondage of trying to qualify on his own for divine favor. Unfortunately, he never abandoned the belief that ethical righteousness was required for final salvation, but he reinterpreted it to refer to the righteousness of Christ that was credited to the account of the sinner. Thus a person was saved on the basis of an "alien righteousness." This continues to be the theological perspective of far too many evangelical Christians who fail to understand the covenantal significance of righteousness by faith as taught by Paul.

Paul's whole theology of salvation is based on the biblical understanding of righteousness by faith, simple trust in the promises of God implicit in the covenant made with Abram and consummated in the Messiah Jesus. God's acceptance is offered freely to all who will receive that acceptance. The covenant established between Yahweh and Abram was based on mutual commitment. Each party was considered righteous, since in the covenantal understanding, righteousness is the status of one who is faithful to his or her part of a relationship.[6]

In the light of this seminal understanding of crucial theological terms, we can make simple sense of Paul's argument in Rom. 3:21-26, a passage that has been at the heart of many theological debates about the atoning work of Christ. If we fail to recognize the meaning of "righteousness" in this context, and particularly if we take the term "justice" (KJV translation of the same Greek word) as referring to "retributive justice," we end up with all kinds of theological confusion.

As we have seen, God entered into a covenant with Abram and his descendants, promising that through them the world would be "put to rights." Since "righteousness" in this context means faithfulness to the covenant promises, we may render it in Rom. 3:21-26 as "covenant faithfulness." But the problem, as Paul had demonstrated in Rom. 2, was that those who were supposed to be faithful had also gone wrong, so the whole world was in trouble (3:23). God's answer was to send his Son, the Messiah, as the one faithful Israelite (hence the "faithfulness of Jesus" is the proper translation of v. 22, not "faith in Jesus"). In sending his Son, God is righteous by being faithful to his covenant word, and in turn, whoever has faith in Jesus is righteous in a covenantal sense because (just as in the case of Abram, the model of this theology) that is the covenant partner's commitment to the relationship. Hence God is "righteous" (not just in the sense of a modern law court) and the "righteousfier" of those who have faith. Von Rad summarizes this relational understanding of "righteousness": "God is righteous so long as he turns towards man. Man is righteous so long as he affirms the regulations of this communal relationship established by God,"[7] that is, by faith saying "Amen" to God's commitment. This is the essence of justification by faith.

Our faith, like Abram's, must affirm the promise, not because circumstances have changed, but simply because God has spoken. We have difficulty accepting this in relation to justification. We want some basis in good works, inherent worth, or potentiality. But its basis is totally in God's grace.

SIX

The Test of Faith, Part 2
GEN. 15:7-18; HEB. 6:13-20

In the last chapter we saw how Abram's faith was beginning to sag concerning the gift of a son. God called him to go out at night and look at the stars, hitch his trust again to the Creator of the heavens, and renew his faith. Abram took God at his word, believed him, and was counted righteous relationally (not morally) because of his faith.

In a similar way, just as God had delayed in making good his promise of a son, there seemed no sign of his fulfilling the promise about possessing the land. Abram was there, but he was a nomad, living among the inhabitants with no real estate to call his own (see Heb. 11:9-10). When his wife Sarah died, he had to purchase a burial plot. So Abram was looking now for some assurance, something to shore up his faith. So he said, "O Lord God, how am I to know that I shall possess it?" (Gen. 15:8).

God answered by telling Abram the most difficult thing most of us have to hear: "You will have to wait." We live in a "now" generation, one that desires instant gratification. We are not emotionally prepared to wait. But God knows that nothing is more suited for character building than developing patience through waiting.

The author had the opportunity to learn this firsthand at a time of major transition. He felt, somewhat like Abram, an inward call to leave the pastorate to attend graduate school and prepare for what he believed was God's plan for the remainder of his life, teaching. But nothing seemed to be working out, and with time dragging on and his impatience mounting, the author kept busy in ministry and found encouragement through the words of the gospel song "Teach Me, Lord, to Wait."[1] It is based on the words of Isa. 40:31: "Those who wait for the LORD shall renew their strength, they shall mount up with wings like eagles, they shall run and not be weary, they shall walk and not faint."

What follows now between God and Abram is one of the most meaningful and exciting events in the entire Bible. Its theological significance informs the entire scriptural teaching about the relation between humanity and God. God gave Abram some instructions that became an object lesson on divine faithfulness. He told Abram to take several animals, cut them in half (except the very small ones), and arrange them in two rows parallel to each other so that a passageway was formed between them, and then Abram was to wait.

We must make it clear that although these actions are similar to making a sacrifice, they are not a sacrificial offering to appease God or to overcome his reluctance to bless Abram. If they were, they would be the kind of religious ritual the pagans practiced! And a proper reading of the condemnation of Israel's sacrifices by the prophets demonstrates that this rationale for sacrifice is foreign to biblical faith.[2] Instead, the actions here constitute a ritual used to establish a covenant relation. Some scholars suggest that the Hebrew word for "covenant" literally means "to cut a covenant."

The way this ritual traditionally worked was as follows: the two parties who were establishing a covenantal relation passed through the corridor between the halves of the animal carcasses. Thus each was symbolically declaring a personal commitment to keep the agreement to the death. In effect, they were saying that if they should break the agreement, they would experience the fate of the animals—that is, if they didn't keep their word, they would die.

What is remarkable about this covenant ritual between the Lord and Abram was that only the Lord, symbolically represented by the "smoking fire pot and . . . flaming torch" (Gen. 15:17), passed between the carcasses—that is, God was pledging his own "death" if he did not keep his promise. Nothing could (or should) have reinforced Abram's assurance of the fulfillment of the promise more than this act of declared self-annihilation.

But this was a covenant between two parties. What was Abram's part? The answer is revolutionary. Abram's part of the agreement was simply to believe God's word, have faith in God's promise. This action demonstrates graphically the fundamental meaning of righteousness or justification we explored in the previous chapter. God was righteous by keeping his word; Abram was righteous by believing it. He was "justified by faith" without any qualifications of moral character or behavior. Here we have the model event that gives theological content to the biblical doctrine of justification; it not only informs Paul's thought but also is the basis for all persons who have such faith to be called children of Abraham.

When the apostle translates these theological truths into the context of the work of Christ, he lays the foundation for a truly Christian and covenantal understanding of the atonement. We, today, have been offered the possibility of entering into a covenant with God through faith in Jesus Christ. The Eucharist thus becomes the symbolic ritual that reenacts the significance of entering into this covenantal relation (see 1 Cor. 11:25). Jesus' death on the cross functions in the same way as the "smoking fire pot" passing through the slaughtered animals. It is God's guarantee that if we respond in faith to his offer of forgiveness and life, we can have absolute assurance that we are forgiven, accepted, and received into the family of Abraham, the family of God. God's action veritably pledges his extinction if he does not keep his word.

SEVEN

The Test of the Vultures
GEN. 15:11

Some city dwellers might have a difficult time envisioning this scene, but those who live in rural areas are quite familiar with it. Many times those large black birds are seen circling over an area like sinister pallbearers, marking the site where some unfortunate animal has wandered into the path of a speeding vehicle. These birds have an important sanitary purpose, but in Abram's case they posed a threat to the consummation of the covenant between himself and the Lord.

It might be exegetically irresponsible to suggest that the author or editor of this narrative was portraying something other than a simple historical event. However, what we are doing in this study is using this event to examine a type of test that often confronts the people of God. In a way it really was a test of Abram that called him to be more than passive about a promise. He had to take action to keep his sacrifice from being consumed before the Lord accepted it. That in itself is an important matter. This test reminds us of John Wesley's struggles with and eventual rejection of quietism.

Quietism is an attitude of complacency toward spiritual discipline and good works. Wesley encountered its presence and practice among the Moravian Brethren after he had been positively influenced by their teaching about justification by faith. Doubtless it was their influence that led to his experience at Aldersgate, where he found the sense of assurance (at least for a time) that he had been seeking since his days as an Oxford student.

The debate that erupted between himself and several of the leaders, such as Augustus Spangenberg and Philip Molther, concerned the meaning of "stillness," the term used for the attitude of "quietism." These men denied that there were "degrees of faith," which meant that there is no faith at all until one experiences the "fullness of faith." A person who is "weak in faith" essentially has no faith at all, they said. Wesley, to the contrary, argued for the validity of "degrees of faith" and that a person could "have *some degree* of it before all things in him are become new—before he has the full assurance of faith, the abiding witness of the Spirit, or the clear perception that Christ dwelleth in him."[1] Such a person, he came to believe, is really in a relationship of justification.

The quietists insisted that until a person had experienced the "fullness of faith," he or she should cease using the "means of grace," such as going to church, partaking of the Eucharist, fasting, prayer, reading the Scriptures, doing works of charity, and giving guidance to others. Wesley asserted just the opposite, insisting that a person could ward off the "vultures" of doubt by taking advantage of all the means of grace. His was a very practical concern, as he found several people who had lost their way, departed the faith, and fallen into sin because they followed the Moravian advice.

What this suggests is that the life of faith must be lived aggressively. The professed Christian who is passive in his or her attitude toward following Christ is in danger of falling far behind in the journey and perhaps eventually getting lost. Oswald Chambers reminds us that "no one is virtuous who is good because he cannot help it. Virtue is the outcome of conflict. And spiritually it is the same."[2]

When Jesus submitted to the baptism of John, he was actually pre-enacting the laying of himself on the cross as a sacrifice, similar to the way Abram laid the sacrificial animals out before God. As the Gospels tell us, the next scene was one of circling vultures. When the Spirit drove Jesus into the wilderness, the enemy challenged him to take some other route than the one he had committed himself to taking at the baptism: to be a bread-giving messiah instead of becoming the Bread of Life through death on the cross; to do some dazzling deed to gain popularity instead of becoming a spectacle of ridicule and dying as a criminal; to submit to some lesser authority than the Father instead of yielding to the Father's will through the agony of Gethsemane.

Throughout his public ministry the scribes, Pharisees, and Sadducees persistently camped on Jesus' trail looking for ways to destroy him, much like a covey of circling vultures. Interestingly he never tried to compromise with them, appease them, or avoid conflicts with them but met them head-on with an aggressive response to their questions and challenges. He even confronted them at times by letting them know he knew what they were thinking and by responding to them.

Similarly, the disciple who sets out to follow Jesus, the "seed of Abraham," is called to lay his or her life on the altar, take up his or her cross, and follow the path of that lonely Galilean. And like the Master before him, the vultures have to be beaten off from the start. It may be the ridicule of peers, the advice of friends not to take this "religion business" too far, or the fiery darts of temptation. Shooing off the vultures takes commitment, alertness, determination, and aggressiveness. Passiveness will almost always result in our sacrifice being eaten up.

No matter how long we live the Christian life, we never can escape the enemy's attempts to have us compromise, lose, or abandon our faith. The vultures take different forms and dive-bomb us with different kinds of viciousness so that we must always be alert and ready to wave them off by aggressively asserting our faith.

Sometimes they take the form of sickness or disease. We all know that we are mortal and that our bodies are constantly subject to being invaded by illness and disease. But when that invasion becomes life-threatening or so debilitating that it drags on and on with no apparent relief, it can stir us to ask, as many do, "Why me?" This can so easily lead to questioning God's love or faithfulness, especially when our deliverance has been the object of extended and earnest prayer.

This test is only one example of a larger issue that God's people have faced through the ages, the "vulture" of disillusionment. Few things are more destructive to faith than failed expectations, and this raises the importance of engaging in a two-pronged attack on the problem. We must carefully examine the legitimacy and adequacy of our expectations and then prepare ourselves to cope with results different from what we anticipated. These factors are graphically portrayed in the poignant story recorded in Luke 24. The Emmaus-bound disciples depicted here are a perfect example of disillusionment. Their hopes had been dashed by the crucifixion of Jesus. Why? They had believed—and hoped—that Jesus had been the Messiah, "the one to redeem Israel" (v. 21). But the problem was real and obvious. Their expectations were based on the popular notion that the redemption or deliverance of Israel would take place by the overthrow of the Romans and the corrupt priestly establishment. Jesus even seemed to foreshadow such an upheaval in his cleansing of the temple. But it did not happen. Things had turned out so unlike what they had envisioned that they did not grasp what had really happened—that their expectations had been realized but in an entirely different fashion. Like almost all their contemporaries, they had misread the evidence and drawn the wrong conclusions.

Unfortunately, there have always been those religious teachers who not only misread the evidence but also propagate the results to their followers, thus setting them up for disillusionment. Perhaps these teachers are sincere, but they still create havoc. An example of this problem occurs when certain so-called prophetic preachers set dates for the end of the world and the second coming of Christ. What happens when those dates come and go? These "prophets" reconfigure the evidence and thus set up their adherents for another failure. The disillusionment that results sometimes brings with it a loss of faith in a truth that has been radically misunderstood.

John L. Peters reports the aftermath of William Miller's failed prediction of the second coming in the mid-nineteenth century. Miller's announcement of the coming event aroused considerable anticipation, with thousands joining the church in preparation for the end of the world. The date came and went, as anyone with any sound knowledge of Scripture could have predicted. According to Peters, the disillusionment resulted in Methodism losing 56,847 communicants.[3]

Most believers have had "vultures" that have attempted to "steal" their sacrifice. It is the common lot of those who seek to be true children of Abraham. Sooner or later all Christians will face situations that challenge their faith and for which there seems to be no reasonable explanation. In such times the only real recourse is to just doggedly affirm that faith. That sounds a lot like Paul's advice in Eph. 6:13: "Therefore take up the whole armor of God, so that you may be able to withstand on that evil day, and having done everything, *to stand firm*" (emphasis added). Maybe Paul should have added one more quality to his fruit of the Spirit listed in Galatians: *holy tenacity*.

EIGHT

The Test of the Dark Night
GEN. 15:12

Like Gen. 15:11 in the previous chapter, verse 12 is probably not meant to be taken theologically; in fact, commentaries scarcely refer to it. But it does suggest a testing time for Abram. To understand the test we must examine it within the larger narrative of which it is a part. The issue throughout Gen. 15 is Abram's quest for assurance. God has made promises, and Abram has yet to see them fulfilled. He has followed the Lord's instructions by preparing a covenant offering and impatiently and aggressively awaiting the divine response. But darkness falls and Abram's experience is one of "dread" (RSV). The question raised here then seems to be, "How is the darkness related to seeking assurance?" The answer no doubt lies in the relation between a promise and the faith of the one receiving the promise. In a word, assurance grows stronger as faith becomes stronger. Conversely, assurance gets weaker as faith becomes weaker.

Once again we may find insight from the experience of John Wesley, whose early religious life was also marked by a quest for certainty. What is remarkable is the similarity between Wesley's means of seeking assurance and the idea of an experience of "darkness." As we will discover, this connection is related to the profound influence of mysticism and the advice of mystics on Wesley in his pursuit.[1]

According to Wesley's own statement, his spiritual quest began in 1725 when he encountered Jeremy Taylor's *Rule and Exercises of Holy Living and Dying*. He was further influenced by the writings of William Law and Thomas à Kempis, a Roman Catholic mystic. His goal, as he stated it, was "to dedicate all my life to God, all my thoughts, and words, and actions,"[2] and the means to that goal was the path of mysticism. In general, the mystic seeks union with God through a series of stages: The first is the *purgative* stage, which is characterized by asceticism and discipline. This leads to the *illuminative* stage, which requires a person to concentrate all of his or her faculties on God. Most mystics would then include a further stage having to do with a *mystical death* in which God withdraws light and forces the mystic to come to God by "naked faith." It is this final stage that is related to our immediate concern.

"St. John of the Cross describes this death as the 'dark night of the soul' where a supreme moral crisis is constituted as the human will completely surrenders to the will of God."[3] This is a theme that recurs throughout Wesley's long career, but under the influence of the Moravians and their Lutheran teaching of faith, he rejected the basic path of the mystic, especially the idea of the "dark night" as an essential stage of spiritual development.

In a letter to his older brother Samuel in 1736, he made a statement that has been frequently quoted: "I think the rock on which I had the nearest made shipwreck of the faith was the writings of the mystics: under which term I comprehend all, and only those, who slight any of the means of grace."[4] The Moravian influence led eventually to his Aldersgate experience on May 24, 1738, in which he initially found the assurance of acceptance for which he had long sought. Tuttle nicely summarizes the implication of this experience in relation to the dark night of the soul: "Aldersgate marks the end of a nineteen-month struggle against the mystical system. Wesley, although retaining a common end with the mystics, substituted an evangelical doctrine of justification by faith for the 'dark night of the soul.'"[5]

This does not mean that Wesley did not allow the possibility of an experience of darkness in the spiritual life, but as Tuttle says, "After Aldersgate it could be demonstrated time and again that for Wesley 'darkness' had its roots in *sin* not in God."[6] To the experience that might be termed "the dark night," Wesley addressed himself more than once, seeking to provide guidance to his followers. In his sermon "The Wilderness State," he explores an experience he compares with the period of Israel's wandering in the desert between the failure at Kadesh-barnea and the crossing of the Jordan into the Promised Land.

Informing Wesley's sermon is the idea that the spiritual life is relational and is sustained on a moment-by-moment basis. The link in this relation is faith from which flows love, joy in the Holy Spirit, peace, and power over sin. These qualities of life in the Spirit are diminished when faith is weak, and lost if faith fails. As we have observed, this understanding implies that every failure of the spiritual life is a failure of faith that in turn is caused by sins of commission or, most usually, sins of omission, specifically "neglect of private prayer" or other means of cultivating and maintaining a vibrant relation to God. *[handwritten: Every minute]*

On this basis Wesley insists that God never arbitrarily withdraws his presence from his people, because "His invariable will is our sanctification attended with 'peace and joy in the Holy Ghost.'"[7] Since God's free gifts are "without repentance . . . He never repenteth of what he hath given, or desires to withdraw them from us. Therefore he never *deserts* us, as some speak; it is we only that *desert* him."[8]

Accordingly, Wesley strongly rejects the mystic teaching that all believers should expect and must experience the "dark night of the soul." "Not only the Mystic writers of the Romish Church, but many of the most spiritual and experimental in our own, . . . lay it down with all assurance, as a plain, unquestionable scripture doctrine, and cite many texts to prove it."[9]

If sin is the cause of this period of darkness, the way out is to carefully discover, by self-examination, the cause and address it. This is the way back to the light of assurance. Wesley does recognize an exception to this principle. If the cause of the darkness is ignorance, the result of the mystical teaching, illumination is the cure and this is accomplished by the proper interpretation of biblical texts that seem to support the erroneous teaching. Wesley also recognizes that temptation can create a time of darkness for those who do not understand life in this "evil world, among wicked, subtle, malicious spirits."[10] The response to this situation is a proper understanding of the Spirit's sanctifying work: "Convince them that the whole work of sanctification is not, as they imagined, wrought at once; that when they first believe they are but as new-born babes, who are gradually to grow up, and may expect many storms before they come to the full stature of Christ."[11]

Although much more can be gained from Wesley's understanding in this area, we have covered several of the most important points. We must now be getting back to Abram and continue from where we left him, in the darkness he was experiencing.

Abram no doubt felt, as darkness fell, the natural sense of insecurity that normally accompanies someone with obscured vision. The description suggests the absence of any light. The comfort of daylight had passed, night had fallen, and so far Abram could see nothing to give him assurance. He had driven off the vultures, but now what varmint under the cover of night might steal his sacrifice! His faith was being tested to the breaking point, but it remained doggedly firm. Then whether at the break of day or in the middle of the night, God spoke. Even if the physical darkness remained, the light of assurance broke in on his soul. Actually, the description of the subsequent events (see chap. 6) appears to have taken place in the midst of the darkness. Eventually, God will always respond to an enduring faith and never leave us in unending darkness. He demonstrated this character in relation to Abram, and he will do the same for the children of Abraham.

NINE

The Test of Patience

GEN. 16:1-15

A small boy* and his paternal grandmother, who lived with the boy's family, would sometimes visit his maternal grandparents, who lived in the country. They would ride public transportation part of the way and then walk about a mile along a dirt road for the rest. On one trip while energetically running ahead of his grandmother, the boy spotted what seemed to be a beautifully colored stick lying in the road. He ran ahead to look and was just about to pick it up when his grandmother caught sight of him and screamed. The "stick" was a copperhead snake, very deadly. Needless to say, the boy kept step with his grandmother the rest of the way.

Like this experience, difficulties—even tragedies—can happen when we run ahead of God's timetable. But that is exactly

---

*The author.

what Abram and Sarai did in the narrative that is the focus of this chapter. The results were disastrous and had lasting consequences. This is the first time Sarai really became actively involved in the developing relationship with God that had engaged her husband. It was to Abram that God had given the promises, although it was understood that Sarai was to be the means through which the promise of a son would be fulfilled.

Ten years had passed since the couple had arrived in Canaan (Gen. 16:3), and there had been no evidence of the promise's fulfillment. Understandably impatient, Sarai came to Abram with the proposal that she give her maid, Hagar, to Abram as a second wife to bear a child. Most interpreters observe that this was a common and ethically acceptable practice in the culture of the time. After all, Hagar was a servant, probably acquired during the ill-fated visit to Egypt, and belonged to Sarai, who could dispose of her as she wished. If Hagar bore a child, it would legally belong to Sarai, and so Sarai reasoned, with a little help, God's promise would be fulfilled. Here is a good example of "the Lord helps those who help themselves" theology.

Right off we see a potential problem from a human perspective. No matter what the culture may have allowed, as a human being Hagar's sense of self-worth was bound to suffer damage from her being used in this way. It will take many years, even centuries, before a person, especially a female person, will be acknowledged as intrinsically valuable and not used as a means to an end.

Similarly, the culture approved the practice of what we today would call "surrogate" motherhood. But here is a case of cultural mores running counter to God's creative intention for the human race. Walter Brueggemann opines, "No moral judgment need be rendered against the alternative device for securing a son, as this may be attested as a proper legal practice elsewhere in the biblical period."[1] However, this understanding is basically flawed because the principle at work is not positive legal or cultural practice but something far more fundamental to human nature. Based on the creation narrative, the divine intention was for monogamous marriage, one man and one woman. Thus, as is so often the case when the structure of human personhood as created by God is violated, unsatisfactory results occur. In this case the result was the destruction of harmony in Abram's home.

The polygamy introduced here continued to be practiced among the patriarchs of Israel with far-reaching and undesirable consequences. While the giving of wives was a common practice when nations entered into treaties, the acquisition of many wives by David and Solomon had unfavorable outcomes. At a personal level, the families involved in these situations were all dysfunctional.

Friction, hatred, and tragedy were certain to result from such circumstances. As H. L. Leupold expressed it, "Polygamy is always bound to be the fruitful mother of envy, jealousy, and strife."[2] This dysfunctional character is vividly expressed in Sarai's response to what developed next. Hagar began displaying a condescending attitude toward her mistress, and this behavior stirred Sarai to jealousy and anger (vv. 4-5). As is so often the case in family disharmony, she blamed Abram for her discomfort, even though she initiated the arrangement (v. 5).[3]

In running ahead of God's timetable, Abram and Sarai set in motion the circumstances of domestic discord. Few situations are more disruptive than this kind of relationship. When one spouse blames the other for circumstances that are mostly his or her own doing, marriage is changed from what God intended it to be. Instead of the the most intimate and happiest of relationships, it becomes a painful union of unhappiness.

It would be chauvinistic to suggest that Abram and Sarai's situation illustrates a violation of some sort of divinely ordained status of male headship. It is true that the "father of nations" (Adam) fell by listening to his wife, just as the "father of the faithful" (Abram) failed in his faith by listening to Sarai. More to the point here is the implication that too often temptation to deviate from God's way comes from those closest to us in our own households. Sarai's suggestion was doubtless made in good faith, but as Griffith Thomas observed, "It is a little surprising that Sarah's quick womanly perception did not forewarn her of these results of pride and jealousy."[4]

Besides the disharmony and hard feelings introduced into the home, long-range consequences were implied in the Lord's description of Hagar's offspring (vv. 8-12). The tension between Ishmael and Isaac that developed continues among their descendants down to the present day. Bad decisions many times have unexpected consequences, often of a devastating character. How much better it would have been for Abram to wait on the Lord in faith to fulfill his promise in his own time!

In his allegory of Hagar and Ishmael in Gal. 4:21-31, Paul draws a parallel between the births of Abram's sons and the circumstances of the Galatians. In this imagery the birth of Ishmael as a potential heir in Abram's family is presented as an alternative to the promise. Ishmael was thus "born according to the flesh" (v. 23) and was a substitute for what God intended, but Isaac was "born through the promise" (v. 23) and was the true heir God planned. Likewise, in the case of the Galatians, they were pursuing an alternative to the promise in their own lives; their temptation to return to the Law for their religious authenticity meant forsaking the promise, which is God's basis for acceptance (vv. 28-29). They were choosing the substitute over the genuine. Like Hagar and Ishmael in this allegory, the Law is the way of slavery, while the way of promise is the way of freedom (vv. 30-31).

TEN

The Test of Holy Living

GEN. 17:1-7

The covenant has been established. God now tests Abram's response to the covenant with two imperatives:

1. "Walk before me" (Gen. 17:1), that is, in my presence. "To walk" means to live life out; life is a walking about. "The verb 'walk' . . . is a reminder that all of life is an ongoing pilgrimage. There can be no 'once for all' formula for instant holiness, because life's circumstances and demands keep changing, like the different phases of a journey. In all of them the Lord wants his people to please him by walking *before him*, that is, in his presence, with nothing to hide from him."[1]

2. "Be . . . perfect" (v. 1, KJV). Most modern translations render this second imperative as "be blameless." One reason for this is that the Greek translation of the Old Testament (the Septuagint) translated the Hebrew word *tamim* by the Greek word *amemptos*, which does carry the meaning "blameless." But

as Steve Green points out, there is a major difference between these two words. "Blameless" reflects a subjective judgment, while "perfect" reflects a condition. Of course in contemporary culture there is a stigma attached to the concept of perfection that encourages us to avoid its use, especially when applying it to ourselves. But as Old Testament theologian Gerhard von Rad observes, the Hebrew word refers to a relational perfection of Abram toward God. It does not necessarily mean moral perfection, or living without mistakes, but signifies complete, unqualified surrender. The word is used in Gen. 20:5 to refer to human relationships "without ulterior motives, unreserved."[2] Von Rad notes that what God is requiring of Abram is the complete, unqualified surrender of his life.[3] Abram is to be entirely committed to God.

Accordingly, the structure of Abram's story suggests four implications of these two imperatives:

1. The holy life is lived out in the context of a covenant relationship. We have seen repeatedly that Abram was not a perfect person as far as being without flaw or failure. He clearly lacked the qualifications to establish a relationship with God on the basis of a holy life. That relationship could only be explained through God's gracious activity that likewise extends to us the offer of communion regardless of our worthiness. In a word, the covenant offered to Abram was a covenant of grace and was established on the basis of God's promise not Abram's qualification.

This was a lesson that took a number of years for John Wesley to learn. In his *Plain Account of Christian Perfection* he recounts that in the year 1729, he

> began not only to read, but to study, the Bible, as the one, the only standard of truth, and the only model of pure religion. Hence I saw, in a clearer and clearer light, the indispensable necessity of having "the mind which was in Christ," and of "walking as Christ also walked"; even of having, not some part only, but all the mind which was in him; and of walking as he walked, not only in many or in most respects, but in all things. And this was the light, wherein at this time I generally considered religion, as a uniform following of Christ, an entire inward and outward conformity to our Master.[4]

In the succeeding years he strenuously pursued this ideal but always experienced defeat in finding the assurance of acceptance he sought. His journal entry graphically described this fruitless pursuit:

> I diligently strove against all sin. I omitted no sort of self-denial which I thought lawful: I carefully used, both in public and in private, all the means of grace at all opportunities. I omitted no occasion of doing good: I for that reason suffered evil. And all this I knew to be nothing, unless as it was directed toward inward holiness. Accordingly this, the image of God, was what I aimed at in all, by doing his will, not my own. Yet when, after continuing some years in this course, I apprehended myself to be near death, I could not find that

all this gave me any comfort, or any assurance of acceptance with God. At this I was then not a little surprised; not imagining I had been all this time building on the sand, nor considering that "other foundation can no man lay, than that which is laid" by God, "even Christ Jesus."[5]

Eventually, under the influence of the Moravian brethren, a group of Lutheran Christians, he learned the lesson of faith that culminated in his transforming experience on May 24, 1738. His own description identifies the link of faith that "closed the circuit" and gave him the awareness of full acceptance:

In the evening I went very unwillingly to a society in Aldersgate Street, where one was reading Luther's preface to the Epistle to the Romans. About a quarter before nine, while he was describing the change which God works in the heart through faith in Christ, I felt my heart strangely warmed. I felt I did trust in Christ, Christ alone for salvation: And an assurance was given me, that he had taken away *my* sins, even *mine*, and saved *me* from the law of sin and death.[6]

Wesley had learned through bitter experience that, as with Abram, God does not scrutinize our moral worth but freely offers himself to us if we will only respond in faith. If this truth is not preserved—and it is clearly implied in the structure of Abram's story—we fall quickly into works righteousness and lose the gospel. The gospel is good news, not good advice.

2. The second implication is that the holy life is lived out in the context of the revelation of a God of power. When the Lord

called Abram to be perfect, he identified himself as El Shaddai, which means "God Almighty." God does not call us to action on the basis of our human capabilities alone. He offers not only the gift of his presence but also the gift of His power. The gospel is good news in this respect also.

But we must recognize that God's power that is effective in transforming human life is not effective apart from our cooperation. Paul clearly makes this point in Phil. 2:12*b*-13: "Work out your own salvation with fear and trembling; for it is God who is at work in you, enabling you both to will and to work for his good pleasure."

This paradoxical statement reflects the biblical understanding of the relationship between nature and grace. On the one hand, if we were to ignore the biblical teaching about the fallenness of humanity, theologically referred to as original sin, we could claim that a human being has the natural capacity to achieve a holy life on his or her own. On the other hand, if we were to adopt a magical view of the divine-human relationship, in which God miraculously changes the structure of the human psyche, Paul's exhortation to "work out your own salvation" would be pointless.

John Wesley quotes Augustine as saying, "He that made us without ourselves, will not save us without ourselves."[7] As far as our five senses go, we could conclude that this paradox is a contradiction. The internal empowering of the Holy Spirit is not perceptible externally; it is known and experienced only by faith. But millions of believers have experienced and testified to this gracious gift of God in their lives. All this is simply a way of saying that holiness of life is a possibility and that it includes the operation of both nature and grace. The twofold aspect of this call to Abram reflects this truth.

3. The third implication is that the holy life is lived out as a response to the faithfulness of God. John Wesley taught that all God's commandments were implicit promises and that by implication the response for which God called would be accompanied by enabling grace. In a word, God's promise is a commitment of himself to keep his word. The faithfulness of God recurs throughout Scripture, giving assurance that when his word is given, we can have explicit faith that it will come to pass.

4. The fourth implication is that the holy life is characterized by "surrender," "openness," and "wholeness." That is the significance of the Hebrew word *tamim*. A relationship of this character is possible only on the basis of a complete trust in the one to whom we surrender. Thus the perfection to which Abram was called is a relationship of perfect trust. Thus once again his faith is put to the test.

Apparently, by this time, Abram's faith had matured to where God's call to holy living did not elicit from him any doubt, fear, or resistance, since he responded with worship: "[He] fell on his face" (Gen. 17:3). The patriarch's name is changed from Abram to Abraham at this point in his pilgrimage—from a name that means "exalted ancestor" to one that means "ancestor of multitudes." As so often in the Old Testament, this change of name implies a change of status that further assures him of the fulfillment of the promise. Perhaps Joyce Baldwin is right in suggesting that "God Almighty is making Abraham a new man, with new power spiritually engrafted. The new name is symbolic of his regeneration, with all the new possibilities this implies." But it could also be an occasion for joking at Abraham's expense, since Sarah was still barren. Faith in the promises of God will often make a person look ridiculous, as it did Noah and as it will do believers in the "last days," who, as Peter suggested, will be scoffed at for their faith in the promise of Christ's return (2 Pet. 3:3-4). Like Abraham, his children must affirm their faith and live in the hope of God's faithfulness.

Both Gen. 15:1-6 and this encounter reveal an advance in the divine-human relationship and a deepening of the understanding on the part of Abraham of what it means to be called by God and to receive God's promise.[8]

ELEVEN

The Test of Compassion

GEN. 18:16-33; MATT. 9:35-38

On the surface, Gen. 18:16-33 describes a strange event. Abraham seems to be giving God a theology lesson on how the Creator of the universe should relate to his creation. He appears to be lecturing God about the way he, whom Abraham had been following, should behave according to his own nature of justice and mercy. In the light of Isa. 40:13-14, one could get the idea that this brashness on Abraham's part was blasphemy: "Who has directed the spirit of the LORD, or as his counselor has instructed him? Whom did he consult for his enlightenment, and who taught him the path of justice? Who taught him knowledge, and showed him the way of understanding?" However, on closer scrutiny, it is possible to understand this event as just another phase in the testing of Abraham to check out his qualifications to be the father of the redemptive race. There may be some significance that this phase of testing occurred alongside an announcement that the long-delayed promise of an heir was now to be fulfilled (see Gen. 18:10).

As we observe Abraham's relationship with God deepening sporadically through the series of tests, we peer further into the intimate depths of spiritual life, a level to which most of us probably aspire but only reach after a long period of growth, if ever. Hence we need to approach this test with deep humility. Here we seem to be seeing the development of those characteristics in Abraham that will result in his being called the friend of God. Oswald Chambers sees the connection in these words: "Friendship with God means that there is now something of the nature of God in a man on which God can base His friendship."[1]

Abraham had lived so close to God that he had absorbed some of the characteristics of God he had experienced himself. Here, in Gen. 18, we see the Lord putting those traits to the test, traits that reached their classical expression in him who was the "seed of Abraham," Jesus of Nazareth. Matthew tells us, "Jesus went about all the cities and villages, teaching in their synagogues, and proclaiming the good news of the kingdom, and curing every disease and every sickness. When he saw the crowds, he had compassion for them, because they were harassed and helpless, like sheep without a shepherd" (9:35-36). Thirteen times we read in the Gospels that Jesus had compassion.

Most discussions of Gen. 18:16-33 enlarge on Abraham's boldness to "[stand] before the Lord" (v. 22) and extol his courage and presumption. Walter Brueggemann refers to it as one of the most daring theological explorations in the entire narrative.[2] But one ancient tradition throws a completely different light on what happened. In this reading of the Hebrew text, verse 22 says, "The Lord remained standing in front of Abraham."[3] You almost get the impression that God is waiting before the judge to see what his decision will be about Sodom and Gomorrah. How will the "judge" respond?

The issue hanging in the balance that is to be decided by the judge is the fate of the two cities of the plain. If we adopt the imagery of the courtroom, we might suggest that God, standing before Abraham, is the investigative agent who is to carry out the verdict of the court. He is first reporting the situation in a way that is similar to the way God is pictured in the narrative about Adam and Eve's eating the forbidden fruit. He does not seem to know, except by hearsay, what is going on until he makes his own investigation. We are not told what he finds, but the subsequent story gives us a sordid picture.

Like many civilizations that have experienced divine destruction, Sodom was synonymous with sexual perversion. Paul's description of pagan immorality in the book of Romans provides a graphic description of such practices. Commenting on the text, N. T. Wright observes that these practices are "subhuman or nonhuman behavior, deeds that are unfitting for humans to perform. Such people are full, Paul says twice, of all kinds of evil; like jugs filled to overflowing with noxious liquids, they are brimful of wickedness, ready to spill over at any moment."[4] Using this analogy, the "jug" of Sodom and Gomorrah was about to spill over. Many modern prophets had drawn the conclusion that if God does not judge contemporary Western culture, he will have to apologize to Sodom.

What would be the response of a legalistic righteousness? It is easy to imagine the call for quick and easy condemnation and annihilation. But by contrast, Abraham manifested a compassion that expressed itself in sustained intercessory prayer. In a similar situation when the Lord had intentions to destroy the Israelites for their apostasy with the golden calf, Moses, too, showed the same attitude. He earnestly pleaded with God to spare his people, even offering to have his own name blotted out of the book of life instead (Exod. 32:32). Paul showed the same self-effacing concern by interceding for his own Jewish people who had rejected their Messiah (Rom. 9:1-3). Only eternity will reveal how many times judgment has been avoided by the intercession of the saints. One of the saddest passages in Scripture is Ezek. 22:30, spoken at a critical moment in Israel's history: "And I sought for anyone among them who would repair the wall and stand in the breach before me on behalf of the land, so that I would not destroy it; but I found no one."

This concept of intercession throws considerable light on Jesus' words to Peter, identified as the "rock" (Matt. 16:18) on which he would build his church: "I will give you the keys of the kingdom of heaven, and whatever you bind on earth will be bound in heaven, and whatever you loose on earth will be loosed in heaven" (v. 19).

But as Abraham's intercession demonstrates, if the recipients of such compassionate praying do not repent, God will not call off his judgment. Although Abraham demonstrated the attitude God wants his redemptive people to display toward those who are in sin and subject to God's judgment, Sodom and Gomorrah still experienced the destruction their lifestyle demanded in this moral universe. —Same today - BOSTON

TWELVE

The Test of Total Commitment
GEN. 22:1-14; JAMES 1:2-8, 12-15

This is the first time the Genesis text actually says that God tested Abraham. While the NRSV translates the word *nasah* as "tested," the KJV translates it as "did tempt" (Gen. 22:1). Not only are both translations possible, but also a significant correlation exists between the two, as the discussion in James 1 makes clear. The Greek word *peirazō*, like the Hebrew word *nasah*, can likewise be translated either way, and both meanings are present in James.

The first chapter of James begins by referring to the "testing" of the recipients' faith by persecution, or "trials" (vv. 2-3), and in the course of James's discussion the message merges into an analysis of temptation. The meaning is clear and very practical. The "testing of . . . faith" (v. 3), by whatever means, can become the occasion for temptation, which is a pressure to give up one's faith in the face of confusion about the purpose of the "trials." That is the real meaning of James's exhortation in verse 5 to those who lack wisdom, that is, wisdom to understand the meaning of the testing. It is not an invitation to ask for factual knowledge without putting forth the effort to learn it, as a student who fails to prepare for an exam might want to interpret it.

This raises the question of the purpose of testing, which *can* originate with God. But as James says, the temptation arises from within (v. 14), since God "tempts no one" (v. 13). Students are tested at the end of a course to determine how well they have learned the course content and to find out if they can apply it. Certain manufactured materials are tested for their tensile strength to see if they measure up for their intended jobs.

Abraham had been through a long course of study with numerous tests along the way to qualify him for the purpose for which he was chosen. Now, as recounted in Gen. 22, God seems to be giving him a final exam, stretching his faith to the breaking point in order to determine his "tensile strength." No matter how one reads the text, because of Abraham's humanity, his testing seems to be an unavoidable occasion for temptation.

The casual reader may think that Abraham heard an audible voice speaking to him, and the text certainly gives that impression (v. 1). We cannot at the outset exclude that possibility. But further consideration will likely lead us to conclude that Abraham probably heard God's voice the same way we do, through an inward impression. This provides fertile ground for Abraham to question the validity of this startling and unconventional word of God. This is like the story of the hiker in the Rocky Mountains who slipped off the trail and was saved from falling to his death by grabbing a small bush growing from the side of the mountain. He called for help and finally heard a voice above him saying, "I can save you if you will do what I tell you." Not surprisingly, the dangling hiker reacted favorably to this offer, responding, "What do you want me to do?" The voice said, "Let go." After ensuring that he had heard the voice correctly, the now desperate hiker asked, "Is anyone else up there?"[1]

Abraham no doubt asked that same question when he heard what God told him to do: "Take your son, your only son Isaac, whom you love, and go to the land of Moriah, and offer him there as a burnt offering on one of the mountains that I shall show you" (v. 2). Sacrifice his son! How can that be? This command was in direct contradiction to God's promise to give him a son through whom he would become the father of many peoples. The Lord seemed intent on taking away what he had given. Thus, in a real sense, to carry out this command, Abraham was being called to sacrifice more than just his son; he was really being called to sacrifice himself. For Abraham, this was a call to end his story, to end the promise he had embraced in faith. Isaac was more than just the child of Abraham's old age; he was the only link to that far-off goal to which Abraham's life was dedicated.

Along with the soul-wrenching agony of sacrificing the life of his son, his "only son," Abraham was also struggling with his basic faith in the God who had been calling him all along and in whom he had put his faith. The God who had made the promise and in whom he had put his hopes is now in fact reneging on that promise. In a real sense, Abraham was being asked to cancel his future.

It is almost certain that none of us will be called on to make such a drastic decision, but actually all of us are called to commit ourselves unreservedly to God. We are called to turn over our futures to him and allow him to shape our destinies and guide the directions of our lives.

This command also calls into question the faithfulness of God. If Abraham goes through with offering up his son, God's word—his promise and repeated intentions to fulfill it—would be aborted. For faith, such a challenge is exceedingly difficult. When we rely on a divine promise, and everything seems to point to it not being fulfilled, the foundation for a wholesale denial or abandonment of faith is laid. Even if a person doesn't abandon his or her faith, such a situation must certainly elicit from that person's lips an anguished cry like that of Job: "Though he slay me, yet will I trust in him" (13:15, KJV).

No one has captured the pathos of this narrative more incisively than Danish theologian Søren Kierkegaard, who has been called "the greatest Protestant Christian of the 19th century" and "the profoundest interpreter of the psychology of the religious life . . . since St. Augustine."[2] Kierkegaard refers to this event in Abraham's life as an "absurdity." He means by this term something that runs counter to human experience and human understanding in general. It is living simultaneously in the infinite and the finite, which defies rational explanation. Kierkegaard insists that we tend to take the absurdity out of this narrative by looking at it through the outcome and thereby miss the impact on Abraham of what he was commanded to do.

In his analysis, written in his unique literary style, Kierkegaard identifies Abraham's temptation as a conflict between a universal and a particular.[3] The universal has to do with the ethical: "Abraham's relation to Isaac, ethically speaking, is quite simply expressed by saying that a father shall love his son more dearly than himself and there is no ethical basis to be found for suspending Abraham's ethical obligation toward his son."[4] Thus in this case Abraham is called to go against the ethical in what Kierkegaard terms a "teleological suspension of the ethical." In the light of the universal ethical principle, Abraham would be called a murderer by sacrificing Isaac, so his temptation is to perform an act that is universally understood to be wrong. But God has called him in this particular case to transcend what is considered wrong to do God's will. As Kierkegaard described it, "By [Abraham's] act he overstepped the ethical entirely and possessed a higher *telos* [purposive goal] outside of it, in relation to which he suspended the former."[5]

The high degree of subjectivity involved here makes it very dangerous to follow Abraham in violating a universally agreed-on ethical standard. Instead we should see his faith as completely implicit and pray for this same measure of commitment to God's will for our lives. In Kierkegaard's terminology, we cannot derive a universal ethical principle from a particular except one of faith in the faithfulness of God to perform his word.

So far in our study of the tests of Abraham, we have not given specific attention to the theological development that reaches its climax in the command to sacrifice Isaac. As we discussed in the beginning, we are generally left to wonder about Abraham's understanding of God at the outset of his pilgrimage. Little if any information is given except that he "heard" a voice. By the time of the present crisis, he has come to know that the God he has been following is God in the most absolute sense. No deity in a polytheistic system could make such exclusive demands of obedience as the Lord has made of Abraham. In many ways God has demonstrated that faith in him excludes any alternatives. "He insists on being trusted only and totally."[6] Here, at the threshold of redemptive history, the foundation is laid for the first commandment given to the children of Abraham: "I am the LORD your God, who brought you out of Egypt, out of the house of slavery; you shall have no other gods before me" (Exod. 20:2-3).

Abraham's faith seems from the narrative to result in a quick and easy response. However, it was probably a matter of much soul-searching, eventuating in a gut-wrenching decision. But he did respond with, "Here I am" (Gen. 22:1). This response is the translation of one Hebrew word, *hinneni (hin-ne-ni)*. Note how the great leaders of the faith were *hinneni* people. This is how Moses responded (Exod. 3:4), it is the same way young Samuel responded (1 Sam. 3:4-10), and it is the response of Isaiah to the call arising from his vision of God's holiness (Isa. 6:8).

Ultimately, with this kind of obedient response to God, any time Abraham called on God, he most likely heard the Lord say, *hinneni!*

THIRTEEN

Preserving the Faith
GEN. 24:1-10; ROM. 12:2

As he drew near the end of his journey, Abraham was no doubt thinking about the future of God's promises for Isaac, the divinely designated bearer of the promises. Recognizing that the fulfillment of those promises was conditioned on faith, he did something that might seem strange in the twenty-first century; however, understood properly the action he took provides an important lesson to those of us who are children of Abraham.

The aged patriarch commissioned his servant to seek a wife for Isaac and gave specific restrictions on the arrangement (Gen. 24:1-10). Specifically, Isaac was to remain in Canaan and was not to be married to a Canaanite woman. How shall we understand this story? Is it merely a custom from a different culture with no relevance to twenty-first-century practices? In the patriarchal period, as earlier described, the head of the clan had complete supervision of every aspect of the lives of those who were in the tribe. This included the right of arranging and approving marriages. Clearly that is a practice without relevance today in Western cultures. Before we too readily dismiss it, however, we might ask ourselves whether our customs are any better at producing lasting marriages.

Aside from the custom of arranged marriages, there is perhaps a deeper meaning. Possibly Abraham gave this commission to his servant because he was well aware of the formative power a community could exert on an individual. During the twentieth century, we passed through a period that reacted against any teaching or practice that restricted an individual from creating his or her own values. Philosophically this way of thinking found expression in certain forms of existentialism, such as the philosophy of the French philosopher Jean-Paul Sartre. Sartre denied the existence of God, asserting that if God existed, he would know what we would do and be and that would take away our radical freedom to be our own creators. But modern human studies have come to realize what biblical faith has always known: who we are is conditioned by the communities to which we belong.

In 1996, adopting an African proverb as the title, then First Lady Hillary Rodham Clinton wrote a book titled *It Takes a Village*. In this book she emphasized the importance of community in rearing children. The proverb had said, "It takes a village to raise a child." Aside from any political implications, with which many disagreed, her point was well taken. Much of the opposition to it was simply a sign of the individualism that still dominated American society. But Abraham knew that if Isaac was to be the qualified perpetuator of the faith, he must be nurtured in an environment that would not erode that faith.

As we observed earlier, archaeological research has demonstrated a thoroughly pagan environment in Mesopotamia, especially in Haran, where the servant was to go to find a wife from among Abraham's relatives. Its polytheistic and pluralistic character was an early version of our postmodern culture. Here is an environment that Abraham feared would negatively impact the promise, so he sternly insisted that his son not relocate to this place.

We now know much about the Canaanite culture. It was a highly developed civilization. Among other things it had invented an alphabet that became the basis for our present one. But it was religiously characterized by immoral Baal worship. Because of the possible influence of this paganism on Isaac if he married a Canaanite woman, Abraham also insisted that this not take place.

Here lies the truth that is relevant to us as twenty-first-century Christians. We all participate in several cultures with their defining value structures. The question is which one is defining who we are, our values and priorities, our philosophy of life.

In 1990, George Barna published a book with the provocative title *The Frog in the Kettle*. In this book he identified the changing characteristics of the culture the church would face in the twenty-first century.¹ The title was taken from the idea that if you place a frog in a kettle of water and gently increase the heat until the water reaches the boiling point, the frog will be so unaware of the changes in its environment that it will eventually be cooked without ever attempting to escape.

The changes Barna described have become reality, as all analysts of Western culture point out. They call attention to significant value changes since the close of World War II. One description says,

> You can take away our jobs, you can close down the churches, you may tear apart our families—but don't ever try to restrict the play time of Americans. Many adults devote greater concentration and efforts to making the most of their leisure hours than they commit to their productivity on the job. Our philosophy and practices related to leisure activity explain much about American perspectives on life, happiness and values.²

Consistent with this image, many pastors are facing difficulties arising from the increasing number of youth sports being played on Sundays. Little League games, soccer competitions, and similar activities that take children and parents out of church can weaken the witness and spirituality of a congregation. One survey finds that the average household spends more money on entertainment than it does on clothing, health care, furniture, or gasoline. Moreover, churches and other types of organizations are finding that a dominant characteristic in today's culture is a lack of commitment. This ethos appears to originate partly in a narcissistic attitude toward life, or a concern centered on what mainly appeals to oneself.

The culture of postmodernity is constantly exerting a downward drag on our lives that we must just as constantly resist. We can learn an important lesson from the experience of astronauts in space. As long as a person is on the surface of the earth, the pull of gravity has to be resisted, thus exercising muscles to keep that person erect. But in the weightlessness of space an astronaut must intentionally exercise his or her muscles to keep them in shape or he or she will be unable to stand when back on earth. Without exercise, the pull of gravity will be too strong for the returning astronaut. Likewise, the "gravity" of the culture around us is an unseen force that must be resisted. But we must gain the strength to do so. How do we do that? By exercising using the disciplines of the Christian life and allowing these means of grace to reinforce our faith and inform our understanding of the distinctive values of the Christlike life.

Because we as individuals are shaped by our culture, what culture should we belong to? The community of the people of God, shaped by the Word of God! As we are shaped by this community, we are more likely to embody the words of Rom. 12:2: "Don't let the world around you squeeze you into its own mould" (PHILLIPS).

EPILOGUE

Like Abraham's experience, life is always a journey. It may be haphazard and ultimately lead to nowhere. Or it may, like Abraham's, have a designated end. Because God created us with free will, which of the two pathways we take is partly up to us. God always places before us a call to realize by his grace the destiny for which he created us. Even if we commit ourselves to pursuing that goal, like Abraham, the journey is seldom in a straight line. Most of us, if we are honest, will admit to experiencing detours and snags along the way. But if our goal is the kind of character God intended for his creation, we will only attain it the same way Abraham did, by the method the Lord used with him. Character is only developed through tests and ultimately by successfully passing those tests. Like Abraham, many of us would admit to not passing every test that comes our way. But if, like Abraham, we keep our eyes on the goal, by God's grace we may more and more clearly reflect God's glory. As New Testament children of Abraham, that goal is the glory of God as seen in the person of Jesus Christ (2 Cor. 3:18).

One thing we need to keep in mind as we think about Abraham's journey, our journey, and the comparison between them is that Abraham was a pioneer. No one had blazed a trail for him to follow; he was the first. Thus while it is easy for us to find flaws in Abraham, recognizing that he took several wrong turns and followed several dead-end paths, we must understand that he was pursuing an uncharted course. We have the privilege of his example and a long history of God's dealings with his creation to learn what wells are dry, which valleys lead to insurmountable peaks, and which passes lead most directly to the destination. Someone said, a bit sarcastically, "The only thing we learn from history is that we learn nothing from history."[1] May it not be so with us!

Although Abraham pursued his goal erratically at times, eventually he came to experience a relationship with God that Scripture refers to as a friendship. Does God need a friend? Perhaps in a sense he does, not because he lacks or needs anything on his part but because he has "no hands but [ours], no feet but [ours]"[2] to embody his redemptive love to his wayward and lost children.

An interesting question concerns what it means to be a friend of God. The term "friend" itself implies certain qualities, but from the tests of Abraham we can identify at least four characteristics: integrity (Gen. 17:1), intimacy (18:16-18), identity of values (vv. 22-33), and implicit trust (22:1-2). Possibly the answer to why God needs our friendship, a friendship marked by these traits, is found in these words of Scripture: "The LORD said, 'Shall I hide from Abraham what I am about to do, seeing that Abraham shall become a great and mighty nation, and all the nations of the earth shall be blessed in him?'" (18:17-18). God needs our friendship to bring his blessing to the nations; he intends to bestow that blessing through Abraham's children, those who have Abraham's faith in their hearts.

The words of Donald J. Wiseman form a fitting conclusion to our trek with Abraham:

> God still desires the close personal relationship with His chosen people repeatedly expressed by Him in the covenant with Abraham and his successors. "I will walk among you and will be your God and you shall be my people" (Lev. xxvi. 12). He still desires that we may respond to Him in faith by calling upon the name of the Lord, as did Abraham (xii. 8). For this privileged relation is now extended to countless peoples "who were once separated from Christ, aliens from the commonwealth of Israel and strangers from the covenants of promise. . . . But now in Christ Jesus you who were once afar off have been brought near in the blood of Christ. . . . so then you are no longer strangers and sojourners but you are fellow-citizens with the saints and members of the household of God" (Ephesians ii. 12-13, 19).[3]

NOTES

Introduction

1. The rationale for the language of happiness used in this discussion is the Wesleyan understanding that God's original purpose was to provide for the happiness of his created beings. In his sermon "The Unity of the Divine Being," Wesley declares, "[God] made all things to be happy. He made man to be happy in Himself" (John Wesley, *The Works of John Wesley,* ed. Thomas Jackson [1872; Kansas City: Beacon Hill Press of Kansas City, 1986], 7:266, hereafter cited as *Works*).

2. Joseph Blenkinsopp, *The Pentateuch* (Chicago: ACTA, 1971), 46-47.

3. See David Clines, "The Theology of the Flood Narrative," *Faith and Thought* 100, no. 2 (1972-73), 128-42.

4. David Clines, "Theme in Genesis 1-11," *Catholic Biblical Quarterly* 38 (1976), 483-507.

5. The purpose of Abram's call defines for the remainder of the Bible the primary meaning of election. It mainly refers to God's choice of someone to perform a task and biblically is not used in relation to eternal destiny. A subsidiary but related use refers to God's election purpose in relation to the character of his people (see Eph. 1:4). See Th. C. Vriezen, *An Outline of Old Testament Theology* (Wageningen, Neth.: H. Veenman and Zonen, 1958), 76, 167.

6. N. T. Wright, *The Climax of the Covenant* (Minneapolis: Fortress Press, 1992), 22-23. No one on the contemporary scene has done more to highlight this biblical truth than New Testament scholar N. T. Wright. He says in his popular devotional commentary on Romans: "Not many Christians, in my experience, make much of the fact of being children of Abraham. We are often content to leave that to Jews, and perhaps Muslims too. Yet the idea of Abraham's multi-ethnic family is important in the New Testament (see, e.g., Matthew 3:8). Is it not time to get this theme out of the cupboard,

dust it down and put it to good use once more?" (*Paul for Everyone: Romans, Part One* [Louisville, KY: Westminster John Knox Press, 2004], 75).

7. N. T. Wright, "Romans," in *The New Interpreter's Bible* (Nashville: Abingdon Press, 2002), 10:399.

8. *The Long Search*, BBC/Time Life Films.

9. Wright, "Romans," 398.

10. John Bright, *The Kingdom of God* (Nashville: Abingdon Press, 1953), 186.

11. Oswald Chambers, *Not Knowing Whither* (Fort Washington, PA: Christian Literature Crusade, 1975), 35.

12. Oswald Chambers, *The Psychology of Redemption* (reprint, London: Marshall, Morgan and Scott, 1955), 5.

13. Aristotle, *Nicomachean Ethics,* trans. Martin Ostwald (New York: Bobbs-Merrill, 1962), 17-18.

14. Charles F. Pfeiffer, *The Patriarchal Age* (Grand Rapids: Baker Book House, 1961), 23.

15. For a conservative discussion of these issues see Donald J. Wiseman, "Abraham in History and Tradition," *Bibliotheca Sacra* 134, no. 534 (April—June 1977), 123-30.

16. Pfeiffer, *Patriarchal Age*, 12.

17. James Muilenburg, "The History of the Religion of Israel," in *The Interpreter's Bible*, ed. G. A. Buttrick (New York: Abingdon-Cokesbury Press, 1952), 1:296.

18. The importance of this point is seen in the light of Gerhard von Rad's observation that most of the patriarchal stories give the reader little suggestion for any authoritative explanation and assessment of any occurrence (*Genesis*, rev. ed. [Philadelphia: Westminster Press, 1961], 168-69).

19. I have chosen, on this basis, to refer to the person who is the subject of these studies as Abram until the time when the biblical text indicates that his name was changed to Abraham (chap. 17). The same is true of his wife's name. There seems to be a significance in these name changes that is directly related to the premise of this work. In similar fashion I have chosen to avoid getting involved in any discussion about the use of the divine name in the Abraham narratives in the light of Exod. 6:3. These are important issues, perhaps, but irrelevant to the point we are seeking to make.

20. I am not suggesting that one can impose an order of salvation derived from Pauline teaching on the life of Abraham or from any other historical sequence of Old Testament narrative, nor am I suggesting that conversely one can derive a structure of contemporary experience from the experience of Abraham.

21. Richard N. Longenecker, "The 'Faith of Abraham' Theme in Paul, James and Hebrews: A Study in the Circumstantial Nature of New Testament Teaching," *Journal of the Evangelical Theological Society* 20, no. 3 (September 1977), 204.

Chapter 1

1. Donald J. Wiseman, "The Word of God for Abraham and Today," Dr. G. Campbell Morgan Memorial Lecture Number 11 (1959), 6.

2. E. A. Speiser, *Genesis*, The Anchor Bible (Garden City, NY: Doubleday and Co., 1964), 88.

3. A. Carter Shelley, *Preaching Genesis 12-36* (St. Louis: Chalice Press, 2001), 6.

4. John I. Lawlor suggests that the traditional view of the only recorded conversation between Abraham and Isaac on the trek to Mount Moriah (the "prediction" of v. 5) is an evidence of Abraham's growing faith in his God and that he was expressing his firm belief that Isaac would either be spared or miraculously raised up, a la Heb. 11:17-19. "As one reviews the complete saga of Abraham, it is to be recognized that several indications of an 'evolving faith' on the part of Abraham do appear; this may be cited in support of this understanding." John I. Lawlor, "The Test of Abraham, Genesis 22:1-19," *Grace Theological Journal* 1, no. 1 (1980): 19-36.

5. Gordon J. Wenham, "The Religion of the Patriarchs," in *Essays on the Patriarchal Narratives*, eds. Alan R. Millard and Donald J. Wiseman (Leicester, UK: InterVarsity Press, 1980), 157-88. Wenham suggests that references to the name Yahweh are chiefly to be found in the narrative framework of the material rather than in the dialogues, implying that the editor or narrator was intending to identify the God of Abraham with Yahweh of the Exodus. This is a much-debated subject.

6. Pfeiffer, *Patriarchal Age*, 86.

7. Chambers, *Not Knowing Whither*, 13.

8. N. Liebowitz, *Studies in Bereshit (Genesis)*, 2nd rev. ed. (Jerusalem: World Zionist Organization, 1974), 113.

9. Ibid., 12.

10. Archaeological evidence concerning both Ur and Haran suggests that contrary to popular opinion, Abram's family was not initially nomadic but lived in a settled city context in both places. Only when he got to Canaan and "pitched his tent" in the hill country did a nomadic life become obvious. See Joyce Baldwin, *Genesis* (Downers Grove, IL: InterVarsity Press, 1986), 22-26.

11. One scholar has suggested that Abram was actually the youngest of the three brothers. This is based on the assumption that the order of names was listed in terms of importance, not age. See W. H. Griffith Thomas, *Genesis* (Grand Rapids: Eerdmans, 1946), 114.

Chapter 2

1. Thomas, *Genesis*, 119.

2. Ibid.

3. Shelley, *Preaching*, 20.

4. Von Rad, *Genesis*, 169.

5. Chambers, *Not Knowing Whither*, 32.

6. By contrast with Abram himself, rabbinic interpretation created elaborate tales justifying and explaining away Abram's culpability.

7. Walter Brueggemann, *Genesis*, Interpretation: A Bible Commentary for Teaching and Preaching, ed. James Luther Mays, et al. (Atlanta: John Knox Press, 1982), 111.

8. William H. Bathurst, "O for a Faith That Will Not Shrink," in *Sing to the Lord* (Kansas City: Lillenas Publishing, 1993), 447.

Chapter 3

1. Von Rad, *Genesis*, 171.

2. Of the "standard" translations, only the NRSV renders the passage this way, reflecting the best of the most recent scholarship and suggesting a much different understanding of the incarnation than the rendering that implies the giving up of "deity" in the enfleshment of the eternal Word. Cf. Richard Bauckham, *God Crucified: Monotheism and Christology in the New Testament* (Grand Rapids: Eerdmans, 1999).

3. Brueggemann, *Genesis*, 132.

4. Steve Zeisler, "The Price Is Wrong," Peninsula Bible Church, www.pbc.org/system/message_files/6922/3973.html (accessed June 15, 2012).

5. John White, *The Golden Cow* (Downers Grove, IL: InterVarsity Press, 1979), 76.

6. N. T. Wright, *After You Believe* (New York: HarperCollins, 2010), 84.

7. Larry R. Helyer, "The Separation of Abram and Lot: Its Significance in the Patriarchal Narratives," *Journal for the Study of the Old Testament* 26 (1983), 83.

Chapter 4

1. Standard formula summarizing the emphasis of the gospel of Luke.

Chapter 5

1. Brueggemann, *Genesis*, 146.

2. Ibid., 116.

3. Helyer, "Separation of Abram and Lot," 83.

4. Chambers, *Not Knowing Whither*, 43.

5. Brueggemann, *Genesis*, 144.

6. For a fully spelled out doctrine of justification by faith based on this biblical understanding of righteousness, see H. Ray Dunning, *The Whole Christ for the Whole World* (Eugene, OR: Wipf and Stock, 2008).

7. Von Rad, *Genesis*, 185.

Chapter 6

1. Stuart Hamblin, "Teach Me, Lord, to Wait" (1953).

2. See H. Ray Dunning, "Sacrifice," in *Beacon Dictionary of Theology*, eds. Richard S. Taylor, et al. (Kansas City: Beacon Hill Press of Kansas City, 1983).

Chapter 7

1. Quoted in Albert Outler, *John Wesley* (New York: Oxford University Press, 1964), 356.

2. Chambers, *Not Knowing Whither*, 36.

3. John L. Peters, *Christian Perfection and American Methodism* (Grand Rapids: Francis Asbury Press, 1985), 118. Ironically, while finalizing this

manuscript a very similar event took place with an "engineer" interpreting the Bible as teaching the rapture would occur on May 21, 2011. As in the Miller travesty, many followers gave away their possessions in anticipation and are now destitute. In one sense, apparently history does repeat itself.

Chapter 8

1. The following discussion is heavily dependent on Robert G. Tuttle Jr., *Mysticism in the Wesleyan Tradition* (Grand Rapids: Francis Asbury Press, 1989).

2. Wesley, *A Plain Account of Christian Perfection*, in *Works*, 11:366.

3. Tuttle, *Mysticism in the Wesleyan Tradition*, 25.

4. Quoted in Theodore Runyon, *The New Creation* (Nashville: Abingdon Press, 1998), 108.

5. Tuttle, *Mysticism in the Wesleyan Tradition*, 18.

6. Ibid., 96.

7. Wesley, "The Wilderness State," *Works*, 6:80.

8. Ibid.

9. Ibid., 84. Wesley's use of the term "experimental" is the British equivalent of "experiential" in American usage.

10. Ibid., 90-91.

11. Ibid., 91.

Chapter 9

1. Brueggemann, *Genesis*, 151.

2. H. L. Leupold, *Exposition of Genesis* (Grand Rapids: Baker, 1970), 2:497.

3. Von Rad describes in detail how this whole scenario reflects contemporary law and custom, including Sarai's comments to Abram: "That [Sarah] does not call Hagar to account but turns to Abraham corresponds to the legal situation, according to which Hagar now belongs to Abraham" (*Genesis*, 192).

4. Thomas, *Genesis*, 148.

Chapter 10

1. Joyce G. Baldwin, *The Message of Genesis 12—50* (Downers Grove, IL: InterVarsity Press, 1986), 63.

2. This discussion and reference to von Rad is based on the exegesis of Steve Green, "An Old Testament Call to Perfection," in *Biblical Resources for Holiness Preaching*, eds. Neil B. Wiseman and H. Ray Dunning (Kansas City: Beacon Hill Press of Kansas City, 1990), 104-5.

3. Ibid., 105.

4. Wesley, *A Plain Account of Christian Perfection*, in *Works*, 11:367.

5. Wesley, *Journal*, in *Works*, 1:100.

6. Ibid., 103.

7. Wesley, "On Working out Our Own Salvation," *Works,* 6:513.

8. Shelley, *Preaching*, 29.

Chapter 11

1. Chambers, *Not Knowing Whither*, 72.

2. Brueggemann, *Genesis*, 109.

3. Ibid., 168.

4. Wright, "Romans," 434.

Chapter 12

1. Story heard by author from Dr. Ed Nash.

2. Robert Bretall, "Introduction" to *A Kierkegaard Anthology* (New York: The Princeton University Press, 1946), xvii.

3. This reflects the contemporary philosophical situation in the nineteenth century and Kierkegaard's challenge to the prevailing Hegelian philosophy that reduced everything to rational explanation by means of a dialectic of "both/and." In contrast Kierkegaard insisted that life entails an "either/or" in relation to which one must make a decision based on an existential leap of faith without objective evidence.

4. Søren Kierkegaard, "Fear and Trembling," in *A Kierkegaard Anthology*, 131.

5. Ibid., 132.

6. Brueggemann, *Genesis*, 189.

Chapter 13

1. George Barna, *The Frog in the Kettle* (Ventura, CA: Regal Publishing, 1990).

2. Ibid., 82.

Epilogue

1. Friedrich Hegel, quoted at "Friedrich Hegel Quotes," Thinkexist.com, http://thinkexist.com/quotation/the-only-thing-we-learn-from-history-is-that-we/534513.html (accessed June 15, 2012).

2. Teresa of Avila, quoted at St. Teresa's Catholic Church, Ashford, Texas, http://www.rc.net/southwark/ashfordstteresa/St%20Teresa%20of%20Avila.htm (accessed June 15, 2012).

3. Wiseman, "The Word of God for Abraham," 20.

BIBLIOGRAPHY

Baldwin, Joyce. *Genesis*. Downers Grove, IL: InterVarsity Press, 1986.
———. *The Message of Genesis 12—50*. Downers Grove, IL: InterVarsity Press, 1986.
Barna, George. *The Frog in the Kettle*. Ventura, CA: Regal Publishing, 1990.
Bauckham, Richard. *God Crucified: Monotheism and Christology in the New Testament*. Grand Rapids: Eerdmans, 1999.
Blenkinsopp, Joseph. *The Pentateuch*. Chicago: ACTA Foundation, 1971.
Bretall, Robert. "Introduction" to *A Kierkegaard Anthology*. New York: The Princeton University Press, 1946.
Bright, John. *The Kingdom of God*. Nashville: Abingdon Press, 1953.
Brueggemann, Walter. *Genesis*. Interpretation: A Bible Commentary for Teaching and Preaching, edited by James Luther Mays, et al. Atlanta: John Knox Press, 1982.
Chambers, Oswald. *Not Knowing Whither*. Fort Washington, PA: Christian Literature Crusade, 1975.
Clines, David. "The Theology of the Flood Narrative." *Faith and Thought* 100, no. 2 (1972-73):128-42.
Dunning, H. Ray. "Sacrifice." In *Beacon Dictionary of Theology*, edited by Richard S. Taylor, et al. Kansas City: Beacon Hill Press of Kansas City, 1983.
———. *The Whole Christ for the Whole World*. Eugene, OR: Wipf and Stock, 2008.
Green, Steve. "An Old Testament Call to Perfection." In *Biblical Resources for Holiness Preaching*, edited by Neil B. Wiseman and H. Ray Dunning. Kansas City: Beacon Hill Press of Kansas City, 1990.
Helyer, Larry R. "The Separation of Abram and Lot: Its Significance in the Patriarchal Narratives." *Journal for the Study of the Old Testament* 26 (1983): 77-88.

Lawlor, John I. "The Test of Abraham, Genesis 22:1-19." *Grace Theological Journal* 1, no. 1 (1980): 19-35.

Leupold, H. L. *Exposition of Genesis*. 2 vols. Grand Rapids: Baker, 1970.

Longenecker, Richard N. "The 'Faith of Abraham' Theme in Paul, James and Hebrews: A Study in the Circumstantial Nature of New Testament Teaching." *Journal of the Evangelical Theological Society* 20, no. 3 (September 1977): 203-12.

Muilenburg, James. "The History of the Religion of Israel." In *The Interpreter's Bible*. New York: Abingdon Press, 1952.

Outler, Albert. *John Wesley*. New York: Oxford University Press, 1964.

Pfeiffer, Charles F. *The Patriarchal Age*. Grand Rapids: Baker Book House, 1961.

Postman, Neil. *Amusing Ourselves to Death*. New York: Penguin Books, 1986.

Speiser, E. A. *Genesis*. The Anchor Bible. Garden City, NY: Doubleday and Co., 1964.

Thomas, W. H. Griffith. *Genesis*. Grand Rapids: Eerdmans, 1946.

Tuttle, Robert G., Jr. *Mysticism in the Wesleyan Tradition*. Grand Rapids: Francis Asbury Press, 1989.

Vriezen, Th. C. *An Outline of Old Testament Theology*. Wageningen, Neth.: H. Veenman and Zonen, 1958.

Wenham, Gordon J. "The Religion of the Patriarchs." In *Essays on the Patriarchal Narratives*, edited by Alan R. Millard and Donald J. Wiseman. Leicester, UK: InterVarsity Press, 1980.

Wesley, John. *The Works of John Wesley*. Edited by Thomas Jackson. 14 vols. 3rd ed. London: Wesleyan Methodist Book Room, 1872. Reprint, Kansas City: Beacon Hill Press of Kansas City, 1986.

White, John. *The Golden Cow*. Downers Grove, IL: InterVarsity Press, 1979.

Wiseman, Donald J. "Abraham in History and Tradition." *Bibliotheca Sacra* 134, no. 534 (April—June 1977): 123-30.

———. "The Word of God for Abraham and Today." Dr. G. Campbell Morgan Memorial Lecture Number 11, 1959.

Wright, N. T. *After You Believe*. New York: Harper Collins, 2010.

———. *The Climax of the Covenant*. Minneapolis: Fortress Press, 1992.

———. "Romans." In *The New Interpreter's Bible*. 12 vols. Nashville: Abingdon Press, 2002.